WHATEVER HAPPENED TO "THE GOOD LIFE"?

or Assessing Your "RQ" (Recreation Quotient)

To Larry & Chris
From Earle
"All life's best!"
P.S. Thank you, Chris.

by
Earle F. Zeigler

Ph.D., LL.D., D.Sc., FAAKPE, RDMRO (Hon.)

The University of Western Ontario

London, Ontario, Canada

TRAFFORD PUBLISHING

2002

i

Printed in Victoria, Canada

National Library of Canada Cataloguing in Publication Data

Zeigler, Earle F., 1919-
 Whatever happened to the good life? / Earle F. Zeigler.
Includes bibliographical references and index.
ISBN 1-55395-047-X
 1. Leisure--Social aspects. 2. Recreation--Social aspects.
I. Title.
GV51.Z43 2002   306.4'812   C2002-904164-3

TRAFFORD

This book was published *on-demand* in cooperation with Trafford Publishing.
On-demand publishing is a unique process and service of making a book available for retail sale to the public taking advantage of on-demand manufacturing and Internet marketing. **On-demand publishing** includes promotions, retail sales, manufacturing, order fulfilment, accounting and collecting royalties on behalf of the author.

Suite 6E, 2333 Government St., Victoria, B.C. V8T 4P4, CANADA
Phone   250-383-6864   Toll-free   1-888-232-4444 (Canada & US)
Fax   250-383-6804   E-mail   sales@trafford.com
Web site   www.trafford.com   TRAFFORD PUBLISHING IS A DIVISION OF TRAFFORD HOLDINGS LTD.
Trafford Catalogue #02-0781   www.trafford.com/robots/02-0781.html

10   9   8   7   6   5   4   3   2   1

DEDICATION

*To my wife, **Anne K. Rogers**, who has brought so much love and joy into our "good life" together*

ACKNOWLEDGEMENTS

I want to express my appreciation and gratitude to my former colleagues and friends, a truly fine group of dedicated professionals, who pioneered the development of municipal recreation in the Province of Ontario, Canada in the 1940s and 1950s. They, and their colleagues in the U.S.A., started us on the road to what municipal recreation is today: a true social phenomenon—an influence for good in a world that desperately needs opportunities for people of all ages, be they in normal, accelerated, or special groups, to enjoy wholesome, creative, life-fulling recreational experiences.

PREFACE

In this book, my hope is that you will find your personal answer to the question that the title asks: "Whatever happened to 'the good life'?" Along the way you will also find an opportunity to determine your own "RQ" or "recreation quotient" based on involvement (or lack of same) in a broad spectrum of recreational pursuits. After doing this and seeing where you score personally, you can then take the necessary steps—if you wish—to raise your Recreation Quotient ("RQ"). Further, this discussion of your leisure-time involvement will be related to society's development.

The "test" or "assessment" of your recreational quotient ("RQ") is based on a scale moving from passive, to vicarious, to active, to creative involvement in life's many educational and recreational activities. It gives you more credit if you are a most interested onlooker or listener rather than a passive one. Additionally, you will score even higher if you actively take part in a particular recreational activity. The highest rating goes to the person who participates in a superior and/or creative fashion.

Why should this subject concern you? It should because one development of modern society has been that people are increasingly crowded together in heavily populated urban and suburban communities. This has created a serious problem. We now need to know how people can find happiness, satisfaction, and a high quality of life despite the increased tempo of living often amidst such badly crowded conditions?

With advancing civilization North Americans have been accused of being afflicted with spectatoritis (i.e., spending too much of their free time watching others taking part in some form of activity, recreational or otherwise). Obviously, this practice is not something that should be encouraged to too great an extent. It is the unfortunate truth that throughout history people in many societies have misused leisure after they have earned it. In certain instances this misuse of free time has actually had much to do with the downfall of that society.

Studies have shown that people are concerned about whether they are getting sufficient pleasure out of life. We know, also, that sound recreational pursuits can add zest and vigor to our lives. The resulting question revolves about whether we will be able to encourage people of all ages to get involved in a variety of recreational pursuits actively and creatively.

We can all appreciate further that there are many ways of looking at the subject of recreation. However, although we could determine averages (or norms) for a given population in regard to types of recreational pursuits followed, it just doesn't seem advisable in a free society to set standards that people should follow.

I firmly believes that a person's value system will—and should—undergird basically any choices that he or she may make about which types of recreational pursuit to follow. Accordingly in the Appendix, you will have an opportunity to assess yourself "socio-culturally" and "philosophically" in this respect.

So there you have it. I hope this book will help to broaden your perspective on the whole question of leisure. I hope, also, that you will consider, and then perhaps even reconsider, this important matter of putting quality recreational time in your life to just the right amount. It's a challenge, of course, but it should be great fun to work it out personally. The "good life" is still out there, but you will have to plan—oh so carefully!—to achieve it. Good luck—and "good planning!"

Earle F. Zeigler
Richmond, British Columbia
Canada

CONTENTS / CONCEPTUAL INDEX

Topic	Page

WHATEVER HAPPENED TO THE GOOD LIFE?

or Assessing Your "RQ" (Recreation Quotient)

1. INTRODUCTION

It wasn't so long ago—do you remember when?—that "the good life" did appear to be on the horizon for all of us in North America. We were urged to be ready for the coming age of leisure. But somehow now we're not so sure about the precise advent of that day. Today, 60 years after World War II, the Korean Conflict, Vietnam, and the Gulf War—and now with a continuing War Against Terrorism, not to mention a variety of other conflicts and social upheaval—intelligent men and women everywhere are taking stock of their status in a world that is indeed destructible.

For one thing, humankind's rapid progress in science and technology in the 20th century, including the capability of nuclear forces for both good and bad, has caused increasingly great concern. This "progress" is coupled with the regression, or dubious progress at best, of human beings in the realm of social affairs. However, we don't seem to hear the warning bells that are ringing to alert us to impending disaster.

In the mid-1960s I sought to look into the future and make a few prognostications about people's use of their free time. I should have known better, but nevertheless decided to make some recommendations to help people cope with a serious problem that recreation professionals and many others felt would soon exist in the "coming age of leisure" (Zeigler, 1967). However, as is the case so often, prophecies and projections are interesting, but they rarely come to pass as predicted. There is no doubt, even today, that "the good life" is here for a small fraction of the world's population. Also, it still does beckon to a slightly larger percentage of the world's population. However, there is also the very distinct possibility that we may all "be dashed on the rocks below" if some drastic measures are not imposed on many aspects of the world's development.

With this cryptic remark I am drawing an analogy with the theme of the famous German poem by Heinrich Heine, "Die Lorelei." In it Heine describes a cliff high on the right bank of the Rhine River at which point the river runs through a very dangerous narrows. According to German legend, a beautiful woman lived on this cliff, and her singing lured unsuspecting sailors looking upward to their death as their boats foundered on the dangerous rocks below. Well, such would indeed appear to be the situation even today, as the human race looks longingly at a promised age of leisure—and yet is unable to cope with the many serious problems and issues of rural, urban, regional, national, and international living.

Of course, we knew that society was facing many problems in the late 1960s, but the feeling prevailed that science and technology would overcome the worst of them in the foreseeable future. The basic premise of my 1967 argument was grounded on the investigation of Michael (1962). His theory was that certain basic assumptions about ongoing social living would continue to prevail (e.g., the weapons systems industries would continue to support a major share of the economy). However, the prediction that the average person in North America would be working fewer hours per week, and would therefore be available to "enjoy life through creative recreational participation," has not come to pass.

As it happened, reported Schor (1992) in *The overworked American: The unexpected decline of leisure*, citizens of the United States today work 320 hours longer each year than their French or German counterparts. This figure represents the equivalent of 40 additional eight-hour days. Schor reasoned that business and culture encourage "workaholism," and he wondered what people can do to reclaim their "rightful" share of free time.[1] (Of course, it can be stated wryly here that today, decades later, many unemployed and homeless people do seem to have more time on their hands.)

In addition to Schor's voice heard above, it can be said further that others have not given up on the idea of people having a greater amount of free time and doing something constructive or creative with this asset. A 1991 section feature in the *Utne Reader* is titled "For love or money: Making a living vs. making a life." In it Edmondson, who wrote about "Remaking a living," quotes Robinson who states, "We are at a point in American history where the value of time to most Americans is reaching parity with the value of money" (p. 69). And this, of course, is not the first time that many in society has become discouraged and disillusioned with only a "work-to-live approach."

Other writers in this feature in the *Utne Reader*, the Whiteheads, Ventura, and Brandt decried people's downward mobility, stated that "someone is stealing your life," and made "a call for shorter work hours, respectively," (pp. 66-87). Interestingly, similar sentiments were expressed, for example, by Lawlor (1993) and Makamoto (1993), the latter referring to a similar phenomenon in Japan. Once again as was stated above, however, Allentuck (1995) in his review of Rifkin's (1995) The end of work points out that the free time for creative leisure will indeed be available—to those who are caught in the throes of what has been called "structural unemployment," an insufficiently qualified group of people who "will find themselves sinking into the permanent underclass" (p. C19).

But then, as if they were writing both a rebuttal and a set of "marching orders" to this ongoing plea, analysts writing a "special report" in *Business Week* (1995) explained how "a radical redefinition of labor" was occurring in "The new world of work." The essence of this argument (or theory) is that company paternalism and guaranteed lifelong employment is out, and that "lifelone employability" is in—but only for those people who are qualified, mobile, well-trained, and self-reliant. Presumably such team-based systems would provide workers with more satisfaction, but nowhere is the concept of "creative leisure" discussed in this exhortation for workers to continually "reinvent" themselves as this "knowledge workforce" navigates along the information highway (pp. 73-117).

The issue of technology's impact on life is a tricky one. Getting to the heart of the matter is not simple. Mesthene's thoughts about technology's role appear in Teich's *Technology and the future* (1990). He decries three unidimensional views about technology's effects that state (1) it's an "unalloyed blessing," (2) it's an "unmitigated curse," and (3) it's "not worthy of special notice" (pp. 78-79). He argues that each of these views has some merit, but he believes each represents an oversimplification of the matter. Empirical evidence can be found to lend support for each theory, but what really is needed, he states, is understanding "about the actual mechanism by which technology leads to social change or significant insight into its implications for the future" (p. 79).

In the final analysis any study of historical change forces a person to conjecture about human progress. After 25 years of research, George Gaylord Simpson (1949) offered his assessment of whether evolution represented progress. He rejected "the over-simple and metaphysical concept of a pervasive perfection principle." He believed that there had been progression, but inquired whether change can really be considered to be progress (pp. 240-262)

2. DEFINITIONS

As you keep your focus on leisure and use of free time, a few brief definitions are in order at this point:

1. The term leisure will be used to explain the time that a person has free from work and does not need for sleep and basic survival activities.

2. It is not necessary to delineate the many meanings of play too carefully; so, I will accept the definition that play is an instinctive form of self-expression through pleasurable activity that seems to be ultimately aimless in nature.

3. The term recreation, often used interchangeably by the layman, seems to have gradually but steadily developed a broader meaning. Typically, recreation embodies those experiences or activities that people have or engage in during their leisure for the purpose of pleasure, satisfaction, or education. Recreation is, therefore, a human experience or activity; it is not necessarily instinctive; and it may be considered as purposeful—but not for its survival value.

4. "RQ" or Recreation Quotient, therefore, is the sum or total of individual recreational experiences a person is having regularly in activities available under each of the five broad categories of recreation available to humans (i.e., sport & physical recreation interests, social recreation interests, communicative recreation interests, esthetic & creative recreation interests, and "learning" recreation interests [e.g., hobbies]).

3. A TEST FOR SELF-EVALUATION OF YOUR "RQ" (RECREATION QUOTIENT)

It is interesting that throughout history many societies misused leisure after they have earned it. In some instances the misuse of free time actually caused the downfall of that society.

North Americans have been accused of having spectatoritis—that is, spending too much of their free time watching others taking part in some form of recreation.

Many people are concerned about whether they are getting sufficient pleasure out of life. Here is an opportunity to determine your overall "recreational quotient" based on involvement (or lack of same) in a variety of recreational pursuits.

This simple, self-evaluative test for adults of all ages was developed so that men and women could rate themselves recreationally and then take steps as they wish to improve their "recreational quotient." There is no doubt but that sound recreational pursuits can add zest and vigor to our lives.

We can appreciate that there are many ways of looking at the area of recreation. However, although we could determine averages (or norms) for a given population as to types of recreational pursuits followed, it doesn't seem advisable to set standards in a free society.

Of course, one development of modern society has been that people are increasingly crowded together in heavily populated urban and suburban communities. This creates a problem: How can people find happiness, satisfaction, and a high quality of life despite and increased tempo of living and increasing crowded conditions?

In taking this test—i.e., carrying out this self-evaluation—please answer the questions as honestly and frankly as possible. The test is based on a scale moving from passive, to vicarious, to active, to creative involvement in life's educational and recreational activities. It gives you more credit if you are a most interested onlooker or listener rather than a passive one. Moreover, you will score even higher if you actively take part in a particular recreational activity. The highest rating goes to the person who participates in a superior and/or creative fashion.

Instructions

Give yourself one point if you answer "yes" to question no.1 under sport and physical recreational interests. In like manner give yourself two points for answering question no. 2 affirmatively, three points for question no. 3, and four points for no. 4. The maximum score for each category is ten points.

At the bottom of each section (or category of recreational interest), total your score from each of the four questions in that section. When you have completed all of the questions in the five categories, total the scores from the different categories.

Finally, rate yourself according to the scale for your grand total, and also according to the scale for individual sections. Although in developing this self-evaluation scale, we did give you more points for active involvement, we are not seeking to establish an overall standard for participation.

After you have completed this assessment and determined your recreation quotient ("RQ"), we will offer some suggestions and recommendations for your consideration. (Please begin now on the next page.)

CATEGORY 1

Sports and Physical Activity

(e.g., golf, bowling, exercise class, walking)

1. Do you regularly at least glance through the sports section your local newspaper?

    Yes ( ) or No ( )... Score _____

2. Are you a faithful follower of at least one team or athlete, rejoicing in victory and fretting in defeat?

    Yes ( ) or No ( )... Score _____

3. Do you take part at least two or three times a week through-out the entire in regular physical activity (e.g., an active game or sport, brisk walking for a mile)

    Yes ( ) or No ( )... Score _____

4. Are you considered one of the better players in any active physical activity or active game or sport among opponents your own age?

    Yes ( ) or No ( )... Score _____

    Total Score for this Section ....Score _____

    Scale: 10 pts.—superior; 6 pts.—good; 3 pts.—fair; 1 pt.—poor

CATEGORY 2

Social Activities

(e.g., social club, church, outing, family recreation)

1. Do you take pleasure in make nodding acquaintances and exchanging the time of day with a number of people?

    Yes ( ) or No ( )...Score _____

2. Do you take an interest in and attend at least one social club or organization regularly?

    Yes ( ) or No ( )...Score _____

3. Do you invite friends in for dinner or a social get-together (or invite someone out) at least once a month?

    Yes ( ) or No ( )...Score _____

4. In the past year have you been elected an officer or served as a committee chairperson of a club or a social or political organization?

    Yes ( ) or No ( )...Score _____

    Total Score for this Section ....Score _____

    Scale: 10 pts.—superior; 6 pts.—good; 3 pts.—fair; 1 pt.—poor

CATEGORY 3

Communicative Activities

(e.g., article writing, letter to editor, speaking, discussions)

1. Do you telephone or drop in on a friend regularly just to pass the time of day?

   Yes ( ) or No ( )... Score _____

2. Do you argue for a point of view even though it may mean a difference of opinion with a close friend or committee chairperson?

   Yes ( ) or No ( )... Score _____

3. Have you in the past six months written one or more letters strongly expressing your opinion to an editor, school principal, or civic official?

   Yes ( ) or No ( )... Score _____

4. In the past year have you given a talk or led discussion at your PTA, church, or any other local group?

   Yes ( ) or No ( )... Score _____

   Total Score for this Section ....**Score** _____

   Scale: 10 pts.—superior; 6 pts.—good; 3 pts.—fair; 1 pt.—poor

CATEGORY 4

Aesthetic & Creative Activities ("Cultural")

(e.g., oil painting, music, sculpting)

1. Do you like to listen to a musical concert or watch a serious drama on television?

    Yes ( ) or No ( )... Score _____

2. Have you attended at least three or four concerts, play, or art exhibits in the past year?

    Yes ( ) or No ( )... Score _____

3. Do you paint, sketch, play an instrument, or sing, etc. regularly?

    Yes ( ) or No ( )... Score _____

4. If your answer to #3 immediately above, do you rate yourself sufficiently high to enter a a content or competition?

    Yes ( ) or No ( )... Score _____

Total Score for this Section ....**Score** _____

Scale: 10 pts.—superior; 6 pts.—good; 3 pts.—fair; 1 pt.—poor

CATEGORY 5

Educational Activities

(e.g., hobbies: ham radio, gardening, astronomy, coin-collecting)

1. Do you like to hear or read about the learning interests of others?

   Yes ( ) or No ( ).. Score _____

2. Are you so interested and knowledgeable in any educational or recreational hobby (apart from one you are engaged in yourself) that you could discuss it intelligently with an expert on the subject?

   Yes ( ) or No ( ).. Score _____

3. Do you have a "learning-interest" hobby of your own in which you are involved regularly?

   Yes ( ) or No ( ).. Score _____

4. Are you considered an expert on your hobby, one to whom others may turn for advice, and possibly having won an award or special mention in the past year or two?

   Yes ( ) or No ( ).. Score _____

   Total Score for this Section...**Score** _____

Now add up the total for each category to get your
GRAND TOTAL—YOUR FINAL SCORE

ANALYSIS

Now rate yourself according to the following scale:

50-35 pts.—Outstanding—*You may be getting too much fun and pleasure out of life. How about doing some more constructive work for a change?*

34-24 pts.—Above Average—*You may have achieved a balance between work and play in your life. You are evidently enjoying your leisure without having a guilty conscience.*

23-14 pts.—Average—*Your score indicate a fair status. You may be somewhat narrow or one-sided, or you may not have achieved much depth in anything. Check this out keeping the ideal in mind.*

13-6 pts.—Below Average—*You are missing some of the good things, the pleasurable activities, that life has to offer. Review and assess your goals for living.*

5-0 pts.—Poor—*Life is undoubtedly a tedious routine for you. Wake up and live!*

RECOMMENDATIONS / SUGGESTIONS

This assessment of your personal "recreational quotient," obviously a subjective evaluation (plus an attempt to be a bit humorous), is based on the premise that you should determine intelligently and carefully what it is that you want out of life. What do you value in your life?

Some might say they want pleasure, knowledge, and prestige, while others might stress creativity, adventure, and good health. A third group might wish for improvement of certain personality traits, a renewal of religious faith, and a continued capacity to profit from a lifelong education.

However you may rank your personal values in descending order, there is solid evidence that choosing a sound educational/recreational pattern in your life is difficult and should be an ever-changing challenge throughout life. The premise upon which this test is based is that the specific decisions you make about which free-time activities you will be involved with— and how you go about carrying them out—can mean a great deal toward the achievement of your life goals.

Some people are lucky enough to have a career in which they can find the satisfactions which coincide with many of their chosen values. But you may not a position where this is possible. This is why it is so important for you to establish your own hierarchy of values and then to select your educational/recreational pattern of living. We wish you well in this quest...

4. RECENT SIGNIFICANT DEVELOPMENTS

It was important for you to go through such a self-evaluation process at this point. Now you have a quite accurate assessment of your present "RQ". So now let's take a look at the current North American situation within a global context to help put your self-analysis in broader perspective. Today we are finding that an unprecedented burden has somehow been imposed on people's understanding of themselves and their world. Even our leaders must be wondering privately whether the whole affair can be managed. What has been going on that makes us worried about the future of human life on this planet?

Before examining the "individual, human recreational experience" more directly and specifically, a brief look at the current world situation should be helpful to our understanding. Such an overview can help us to broaden our outlook and gain some insight into our problems. So let us consider some recent developments in society at large to help put our North American situation in even better perspective.

Do Difficult Days Lie Ahead for North Americans?

North Americans, generally speaking, still do not fully comprehend that our unique position in the history of the world's development will in all probability change radically in the 21st century. The years ahead are really going to be difficult ones for us all. The United States, as the one major nuclear power, will have the ongoing, overriding problem of maintaining large-scale peace at least. (Of course, a variety of countries may or may not have nuclear arms capability, and that is what is so worrisome as well.) Additionally, along with other leading countries, there are severe ecological problems, a worldwide nutritional problem, the ebbs and flows of an energy crisis, and a situation where the rising expectations of the underdeveloped nations—including their staggering debt—will somehow have to be met, to name just a few of the major concerns.

Indeed, although it is seemingly more true of the United States than Canada, history is going against us in several ways. This means that previous optimism must be tempered to shake us loose from delusions, some of which we still have. For example, despite the presence of the United Nations, the United States has persisted in envisioning itself—the world's only superpower!—as almost being endowed by the Creator to make all crucial political decisions. Such decisions, often to act unilaterally with the hoped-for belated sanction of the United Nations, have resulted in United States-led incursions in the Middle East in the two wars and into Somalia for very different reasons. There are other similar situations on the recent horizon (e.g., the former Yugoslavia, Rwanda, Sudan, and Haiti, respectively)—not to mention the present War on Terrorism. This most recent "war," of course, will be a never-ending one!

Accordingly, there should soon be reason to expect selected U.S. retrenchment brought on by its excessive world involvement and staggering debt. Of course, any such retrenchment would inevitably lead to a decline in the economic and military influence of the United States. But who can argue logically that the present uneasy balance of power is a healthy situation looking to the future. Norman Cousins appears to have sounded just the right note a generation ago when he stated that perhaps "the most important factor in the complex equation of the future is the way the human mind responds to crisis" (1974, 6-7). The world culture as we know it must respond adequately to the many challenges with which it is being confronted. The societies and nations must individually and collectively respond positively, intelligently, and strongly if humanity as we have known it is to survive.

These Developments Have "Transformed Our Lives"

Continuing this discussion of international developments and the possible achievement of historical perspective, we should also keep in mind the significant developments of the decades immediately preceding the 21st century. For example, Naisbitt (1982) outlined the "ten new directions that are transforming our lives," as well as the "megatrends" apparent because of women's evolving role in societal structure (Aburdene & Naisbitt, 1992). Here I am referring to:

1. the concepts of the information society and INTERNET,

2. "high tech/high touch,"

3. the shift to world economy,

4. the need to shift to long-term thinking in regard to ecology,

5. the move toward organizational decentralization,

6. the trend toward self-help,

7. the ongoing discussion of the wisdom of participatory democracy as opposed to representative democracy,

8. a shift toward networking,

9. a reconsideration of the "North-South" orientation, and

10. the viewing of decisions as "multiple option" instead of "either/or"

Add to this the ever-increasing, lifelong involvement of women in the workplace, politics, sports, organized religion, and social activism. Now we can finally begin to understand that a new world order has descended upon us as we move along into the 21st century.

Moving ahead in time slightly past Naisbitt's first set of *Megatrends,* as well as the 1992 set of Aburdene & Naisbitt, a second list of 10 issues facing political leaders was highlighted in the mid-1990s in the *Utne Reader* titled "Ten events that shook the world between 1984 and 1994" (1994, pp. 58-74). Just consider the following:

1. the fall of communism and the continuing rise of nationalism,

2. the environmental crisis and the "green movement,"

3. the AIDS epidemic and the "gay response,"

4. many continuing wars and the peace movement,

5. the gender war,

6. religion and racial tension,

7. the concept of "West meets East" and resultant implications,

8. the "Baby Boomers" came of age and "Generation X" has started to worry and complain because of declining expectation levels,

9. the whole idea of globalism and international markets, and, finally,

10. the computer revolution and the spectre of Internet.

The World Has Three Major Trading Blocks Now

Keeping the above in mind, the world's "economic manageability" may have been helped by its division into three major trading blocs: (1) the Pacific Rim dominated by Japan, (2) the European Community very heavily influenced by Germany, and (3) North America dominated by the United States of America. While this appears to be true to some observers, interestingly perhaps something even more fundamental has occurred. Succinctly put, world politics seems to be "entering a new phase in which the fundamental source of conflict will be neither ideological nor economic." In the place of these Samuel P. Huntington, of Harvard's Institute for Strategic Studies, believes that now the major conflicts in the world will actually be clashes between different groups of civilizations espousing fundamentally different cultures *(The New York Times*, June 6, 1993, E19).

These clashes, Huntington states, represent a distinct shift away from viewing the world as being composed of first, second, and third worlds as was the case during the Cold War. Thus, Huntington is arguing that in the 21st century the world will return to a pattern of development evident several hundred years ago in which civilizations will actually rise and fall. (Of course, this is exactly what was postulated by the late Arnold Toynbee in his earlier famous theory of historical development.)

Thus, internationally, with the dissolution of the Union of Soviet Socialist Republics (USSR), Russia and the remaining communist regimes are being severely challenged as they seek to convert to more of a capitalistic economic system. Additionally, a number of other multinational countries are showing signs of potential break-ups (e.g., Yugoslavia, China, Canada). Further, the evidence points to the strong possibility that the developing nations are becoming ever poorer and more destitute with burgeoning populations and widespread starvation setting in.

Further, Western Europe is facing a demographic time bomb even more than the United States because of the influx of refugees from African and Islamic countries, not to mention refugees from countries of the former Soviet Union and Africa. It appears further that the European Community will be inclined to appease Islam's demands. However, the multinational nature of the European Community will tend to bring on economic protectionism to insulate its economy against the rising costs of prevailing socialist legislation.

Still further, there is some evidence that Radical Islam, along with Communist China, may become increasingly aggressive toward the Western culture of Europe and North America. (Note: This has become true since this prediction was made originally.) At present, Islam gives every evidence of replacing Marxism as the world's main ideology of confrontation. For example, Islam is dedicated to regaining control of Jerusalem and to forcing Israel to give up land occupied earlier as a buffer zone against Arab aggressors. Also, China has been arming certain Arab nations, but how can we be too critical in this regard when we recall that the U.S.A. has also been arming selected countries when such support was deemed in its interest.

As Hong Kong is absorbed into Communist China, further political problems seem inevitable in the Far East as well. Although North Korea is facing agricultural problems, there is the possibility (probability?) of the building of nuclear bombs there. (Further, there is the ever-present fear worldwide that small nations and terrorists will somehow get nuclear weapons too.) A growing Japanese assertiveness in Asian and world affairs also seems inevitable because of its extremely strong financial position. Yet the flow of foreign capital from Japan into North America has slowed down somewhat because Japan is being confronted with its own financial crisis caused by inflated real estate and market values. There would obviously be a strong reaction to any fall in living standards in this tightly knit society. Interestingly, still further, the famed Japanese work ethic has become somewhat tarnished by the growing attraction of leisure opportunities.

The situation in Africa has become increasingly grim because the countries south of the Sahara Desert (i.e., the dividing line between black Africa and the Arab world) have experienced extremely bad economic performance in the final quarter of the 20th century. This social influence has brought to a halt much of the continental effort leading to political liberalization while at the same time exacerbating traditional ethnic rivalries. This economic problem has accordingly forced governmental cutbacks in many of the countries because of the pressures brought to bear by the financial institutions of the Western world that have been underwriting much of the development that had taken place. The poor are therefore getting poorer, and health and education standards have in many instances deteriorated even lower than they were previously. Finally, the increasing AIDS epidemic "hovers" over it all

5. THE IMPACT OF NEGATIVE SOCIAL FORCES HAS INCREASED

Shifting the focus of this discussion from the problems of an unsettled "Global Village" back to the problem of "living the good life" in the 21st century in North America, we are now finding that the human recreational experience will have to be earned typically within a society whose very structure has been modified. For example, the concept of the traditional family structure has been strongly challenged by a variety of social forces (e.g., economics, divorce rate); many single people are finding that they must work longer hours; and many families need more than one breadwinner just to make ends meet. Also, the idea of a steady surplus economy may have vanished, temporarily it is hoped, in the presence of a substantive drive to reduce a budgetary deficit by introducing major cutbacks in so-called non-essentials.

The Problems of Megalopolis Living Have Not Yet Been Solved

Additionally, many of the same problems of megalopolis living described in 1967 still prevail and are even increasing (e.g., declining infrastructure, crime rates (some of them anyhow), transportation gridlocks, overcrowded schools). Interestingly, in that same year of 1967, Prime Minister Lester Pearson asked Canadians to improve "the quality of Canadian life" as Canada celebrated her 100th anniversary as a confederation. And still today, despite all of the current identity problems, Canada can take pride in that it been consistently proclaimed as one of the best places on earth to live (with the United States not very far behind). Nevertheless, we can't escape the fact that the work week is not getting shorter and shorter— and that Michaels' prediction about four different types of leisure class still seems a distant dream for the large majority of people.

Further, the situation has developed in such a way that the presently maturing generation, so-called Generation X, is finding that fewer good-paying jobs are available and the average annual income is declining. What caused this to happen? This is not a simple question to answer. For one thing, despite the rosy picture envisioned a generation ago, one in which we were supposedly entering a new stage for humankind, we are unable today to cope adequately with the multitude of problems that have developed. This is true whether inner city, suburbia, exurbia, or small-town living are concerned. Transportation jams and gridlock, for example, are occurring daily as public transportation struggles to meet rising demand for economical transport within the framework of developing megalopolises.

Megalopolis living trends have certainly not abated and will probably not do so in the predictable future. More and more families, where that unit is still present, need two breadwinners just to survive. Interest rates fluctuate but remain reasonably high, thereby discouraging many people from home ownership. Pollution of air and water continues despite efforts of many to change the present course of development. High-wage industries seem to be "heading south" in search of places where lower wages can be paid. Also, all sorts of crime are still present in our society, a goodly portion of it seemingly brought about by unemployment and rising debt at all levels from the individual to the federal government.

The rise in youth crime is especially disturbing. In this respect, we are fortunate that municipal, private-agency, and public recreation has received continuing financial support from the increasingly burdened taxpayer.

What Character Do We Seek for Our People?

Further, we North Americans, functioning within this world that has nevertheless become a "Global Village" communications-wise, need to think more seriously than ever before about the character and traits for which we should seek to develop in our people. We can only continue to lead or to strive for the proverbial good life if children and young people develop the right attitudes (psychologically speaking) toward education, work, use of leisure, participation in government, various types of consumption, and concern for world stability and peace.. Make no mistake about it: if we truly desire "the good life," education for the creative and constructive use of leisure, as a significant part of ongoing general education, should have a unique role to play now and forever more.

The Old World countries all seem to have a "character"; it is almost something that they take for granted. Do we have what can be called a character in North America (i.e., in the United States, in Canada)? Americans were thought earlier to be heterogeneous and individualistic as a people, as opposed to Canadians. But the Canadian culture has changed significantly in recent decades as people, feeling welcome because of Canada's planned multiculturalism, began to arrive from many different lands . And, of course, Canada was founded originally by two distinct cultures, the English and the French.

Schlesinger (1998), in his revised analysis of the American situation, writes with considerable concern about "the disuniting of America." Speaking about Canada, also, he asks, "If one of the top five developed nations on earth can't make a federal, multi-ethnic state work, who else can?" His response: "The answer to that increasingly vital question has been, at least until recently, the United States" (p. 14). What he is saying is that Canada has been going about multi-culturalism the wrong way for some time—and that the United States had presumably been working earlier toward a "melting-pot" development, but somehow is now moving in the same direction as Canada!

In retrospect, shortly after the middle of the 20th century, Commager (1966), the noted historian, enumerated what he believed were some common denominators in the American character. These, he said, were:

    1. carelessness;

2. openhandedness, generosity, and hospitality;

3. self-indulgence;

4. sentimentality, and even romanticism;

5. gregariousness;

6. materialism;

7. confidence and self-confidence;

8. complacency, bordering occasionally on arrogance;

9. cultivation of the competitive spirit;

10. indifference to, and exasperation with laws, rules, and regulations;

11. equalitarianism; and

12. resourcefulness (pp. 246-254).

What about Canadian character as opposed to what Commager stated above? To help us in this regard, Lipset (1973) earlier made a perceptive comparison between the two countries. After stating that they probably resemble each other more than any other two countries in the world, he did assert that there seems to be a rather "consistent pattern of differences between them" (p. 4). He found that certain "special differences" did exist and may be singled out as follows:

> Varying origins in their political systems and national identities, varying religious traditions, and varying frontier experiences. In general terms, the value orientations of Canada stem from a counterrevolutionary past, a need to differentiate itself from the United States, the influence of Monarchical institutions, a dominant Anglican religious tradition, and a less individualistic and more governmentally controlled expansion of the Canadian than of the American frontier (p. 5).

Lipset's findings tend to sharpen the focus on opinions commonly held earlier that, even though there is considerable sharing of values, they are held more tentatively in Canada. Also, he believed that Canada has consistently settled on "the middle ground" between positions arrived at in the United States and England. However, Lipset argued that, although the twin values of equalitarianism and achievement have been paramount in American life, but somewhat less important in Canada, there was now consistent movement in this direction in Canada as well (p. 6).

6. WHAT HAPPENED TO THE ORIGINAL ENLIGHTENMENT IDEAL?

The achievement of "the good life" for a majority of our citizens in North America, a good life that involves a creative and constructive use of leisure as a key part of continuing general education, necessarily implies that a certain type of progress has been made in society. However, we should understand that our chief criterion of progress has undergone a subtle but decisive change since the founding of the United States republic. This development has had a definite influence on Canada and Mexico as well. Such change has been at once a cause and a reflection of some of our current disenchantment with technology. Recall that the late 18th century was a time of political revolution when monarchies, aristocracies, and the ecclesiastical structure were being challenged on a number of fronts. Also, the factory system was undergoing significant change at that time. Such industrial development with its greatly improved machinery "coincided with the formulation and diffusion of the modern Enlightenment idea of history as a record of progress. . . ." (Marx, 1990, p. 5). (This is obviously not *the* Karl Marx!)

Thus, this "new scientific knowledge and accompanying technological power was expected to make possible a comprehensive improvement in all of the conditions of life—social, political, moral, and intellectual as well as material." This idea did indeed slowly take hold and eventually "became the fulcrum of the dominant American worldview" (Marx, p. 5). By 1850, however, with the rapid growth of the United States especially, the idea of progress was already being dissociated from the Enlightenment vision of political and social liberation.

Technology and Life Improvement

By the turn of the twentieth century, "the technocratic idea of progress [had become] a belief in the sufficiency of scientific and technological innovation as the basis for general progress" (Marx, p. 9). This came to mean that if scientific-based technologies were permitted to develop in an unconstrained manner, there would be an automatic improvement in all other aspects of life! What has happened—because this theory became coupled with onrushing, unbridled capitalism—was that the ideal envisioned by Thomas Jefferson haa been turned upside down. Instead of social progress being guided by such values as justice, freedom, and self-fulfillment for all people, rich or poor, these goals of vital interest in a democracy were subjugated to a burgeoning society dominated by supposedly more important instrumental values—that is. those values that would be useful or practical ones for advancing a capitalistic system!

So the fundamental question still today is, "which type of values will win out in the long run?" In North America, also, it seems that a gradually prevailing concept of cultural relativism will be increasingly discredited since the 1990s witnessed a sharp clash between (1) those who uphold so-called Western cultural values and (2) those who by their presence are dividing the West along a multitude of ethnic and racial lines. This is occasioning strong efforts to promote fundamentalistic religions and sects—either those present historically or those recently imported. These numerous religions, and accompanying sects, are characterized typically by decisive right/wrong morality.

7. THE ECONOMIC SITUATION

The economic situation in North America is creating a great many problems as well. Massive budget deficits at the national and state or provincial levels—with occasional efforts to become solvent—are bringing forth all sorts of "creative" solutions, solutions basically promulgated as a result of conflicting economic theories. Tax burdens on consumption will no doubt tend to increase tax revolts throughout North America as household wealth declines, credit-card debt mounts, and the number of personal and business bankruptcies rises.

The economic status of the countries to the north and south of the United States, Canada and Mexico, respectively, has been a problem as well. As these words are being written, the Canadian dollar is hovering around 64 cents U.S., a far cry from the days when it was higher than its counterpart (i.e., 1971). However, some economists and financiers are optimistic that in due time it will strengthen further, while others see a 50-cent Canadian dollars as "soon-to-be-achieved" certainty. Thus, talk is heard that it is time for currency similar to the "Euro dollar" in North America. Significantly, also, Mexico has been able to meet its repayment schedule on money borrowed from the United States. Further, despite agreement on the subject of what is being called "free trade," the North American Free Trade Agreement in the final analysis leaves much to be desired. Change is needed to a substantive degree.

However, unemployment is proving most difficult to bring under control. Yet any undue protectionism would undoubtedly retard economic free trade. In Canada free trade really doesn't even exist among the various provinces! Since NAFTA was approved, the need for job creation at the governmental level has grown as the "free trade concept" moves from north to south proceeding from Canada to Mexico (and who knows where else in the world). As indicated above, social entitlements to citizens (e.g., social security, Medicare, Medicaid), including the "welfare state concept" will evidently continue to be challenged severely.

Also, as the United States seeks to develop health-care standards for all, and Canada struggles to retain those that it has, citizens will eventually face higher taxes of varying types in an effort to maintain the health-care bill as well as to reduce the debt at all levels at the same time. Some say a two-tier health-care system is inevitable in Canada. At present in the USA, the Republican-dominated Congress—with the help of certain Democrats—is holding back the growth of a public health-care system and other entitlements while at the same time offering a tax cut. How this will play out in the long run is anybody's guess. Canada has also been facing serious financial problems with its ballooning national debt and a devalued dollar. This situation is exacerbated by the fact that its level of social benefits have tradionally been somewhat higher than those of the United States.

These developments all have import for older citizens; retirement at age 65, especially early retirement at 55, may still be available (e.g., the "Golden Handshake"), but government, businesses, and people themselves will find it necessary to keep people working longer to pay the requisite taxes required to pay all of the bills. Yet, statistics reveal that the rich are still getting richer, and the poor are still getting poorer! "Workfare" seems destined for greater implementation. However, for those who can escape, the migration away from the big cities will continue as the various types of infrastructures continue to deteriorate along with the other negative aspects of urban living.

The Relationship Between a Surplus Economy and the Availability of Leisure

What does all of the above mean in regard to the availability of leisure. As mentioned earlier, a surplus economy is needed before leisure can become available to even a minority of the world's populations. Thus, the sooner economic theory points the way for society to maintain a steady, surplus economy, the sooner there will be the possibility of an increasing percentage of the total population having more free time. When, or if, this halcyon day ever arrives, we can then expect an increasing amount of pressure being exerted upon people to use their leisure wisely.

8. THE STATUS OF EDUCATION

Now shift your focus momentarily from the economic problems of society in general, and the direct relationship of prosperity to the general availability of leisure, to that of education in particular. If the status of public education is not sound, how can we ever expect to promote "education for the creative use of leisure?" Depending on one's educational philosophy, the revised picture that we see in education today is complex and is also definitely disheartening to many. The clamor of the early 1960s for improvement that followed the U.S.S.R.'s first Sputnik was followed by the passivity of the 1970s. The situation heated up again to a considerable degree in the 1980s at the various educational levels mainly because of competitive demands for the tax dollar. However, despite the clamor for higher educational standards in the 1990s, my own analysis of the situation is that we have simply lost track of—if we ever knew—what the best type of education is—that is, what curriculum and what teaching methodology should be employed in keeping with the democratic ideals that are so glibly espoused.

I note also what I believe is an unwise thrust toward school privatization caused by declining scores in typically narrowly defined tests. Yet, I can understand that people are justifiably concerned about the provision of safer environments for their children as the breakdown of public order continues in this basic social institution. Since it is now legal to carry a concealed weapon in more than half of the states in the United States, keeping weapons out of schools has becoming a highly vexing problem. Canada has its problems too, of course, to name one—the ongoing effort to break up the country by a significant percentage of Francophones. How this issue will be resolved ultimately is anyone's guess at present.

Granting the presence of pluralistic philosophies of education in democratic countries, the deficiencies of the educational system, often based on inadequate curriculum content and instructional methodology, point up the present inability to provide people with a lifelong educational pattern. This statement applies both to the results of the provision of general education to all, as well as to the best type of professional education. Assuredly, some of the complaints of the 1960s have been rectified to an extent, but now—as so often happens—the pendulum has again swung in the wrong direction. I believe this is true (1) because the evident "return to essentials" is based completely on what has been called a "logical" as opposed to a "psychological" order of learning; (2) because in the present environment social science and humanities-oriented subjects tend to be downgraded along with music and art in the curriculum; and (3) because music, art, and developmental physical activity in sport, exercise, and related activities are relegated by many to a tertiary level.

A "Return-to-Essentials" Approach Prevails

As stated, this "return-to-essentials" educational philosophy is undoubtedly prevailing, especially insofar as the hard sciences and mathematics are concerned. I agree that we must do better in these areas, but I am anxious to see this improvement spread across the humanities, social sciences, and natural sciences relatively evenly. In each area I believe we need to spell out precisely what knowledge, competencies, and skill are required for optimum living in today's world. Once this is done, we should then provide laboratory experiences in each area to guarantee that minimum achievement has been attained at the various levels along the way.

Approaching the situation from a broader perspective, it could be argued that much of the current problem stems from the fact that education is faced with almost insurmountable problems. I believe this to be true, because other basic societal institutions (e.g., the church, the family) are floundering. The school's burden is being increased to fill these gaps— deficiencies that could be made up largely if we had the funds and the attitudinal support to implement a competency-based approach to the needed knowledge and skills required for adequacy in life mastery in the 21st century.

Additionally, the educational infrastructure needs approximately 200 billion dollars (plus!) put into it to bring it up to par. I could go on, but this situation is well known. I am most concerned about the stupidity, illogicality, greed, and lack of foresight evident all about us, not to mention what appears to be ever-present evil! However, I know we as individuals must work these things out for ourselves by being more vigorously melioristic, and not by displaying blind pessimism or "Polyannish" optimism. It is indeed going to be unbelievably difficult—i.e., dragging literally billions of people "kicking and screaming in all directions" into the 21st century.

In addition to education at all levels taking a beating—often undeserved—within this structure, sound physical education and truly recreational sport are, in turn, once again facing crises from without and within. Overemphasized, commercialized sport carried out by misguided administrators, players, coaches, and officials in professional leagues, the programs in a significant percentage of misguided universities (including too many high schools!), and the Olympic Games, each viewed typically by seemingly bewitched spectators, deserve whatever oblivion may eventually befall it! A social institution such as this dubious type of sporting competition—that actually does more harm than good—should be eliminated. Competitive sport that is not "sportspersonlike" and uplifting has no legitimate place in society, much less in the educational system or community recreation programming. Sport must not be used to enable ever-more aggressive capitalism!

Physical Education, Art, and Music Are Still Struggling for Recognition

My own profession of physical education/kinesiology has been fighting an uphill struggle since well before I entered the field more than half a century ago. I fully appreciate that progress is never a straight-line affair. I understand also that the pendulum does swing to the right and the left and never seems to stop in the middle. So now, as I am of necessity winding down my years in the field, the situation is *still* that physical education—and art and music too—are facing a severe, uphill struggle. Frankly, I believe that we deserve a better fate. The scientific evidence is mounting daily about the beneficial effects of regular, well-taught, and well-conceived programs of development physical activity. Yet, sadly, where physical education once was largely required, it is now often fighting to remain as an elective offering within the many elementary, middle, and secondary schools. This is also the case in our colleges and universities in the many states and provinces. And yet, as mentioned immediately above, we also have ever-stronger evidence through ongoing investigation that, in addition to enabling a person to live life more fully, steady involvement in the right kind of developmental physical activity will actually help a person to live longer. Moreover, in the case of people from 65 to 85 years of age, an "irreducible-minimum" level of fitness will go a long way toward helping them remain independent and self-sufficient!

9. PUTTING LEISURE IN HISTORICAL PERSPECTIVE

A basic premise of this essay is that a sufficient amount of leisure is a requirement for the good life. A second basic premise is that a democratic society should foster an ideal use of leisure. Let us grant that it may well be impossible to gain objectivity or true historical perspective on the rapid world change that is taking place. However, we may well ask, also, why it took so long—that is, so many hundreds of years—before the possibility of earning and using leisure became a reality—at least to some degree—for the average North American.

This is not a simple question to answer. In the first place, it could be argued that this possibility has really come quite rapidly considering the length of times that the human has been developing on earth. Also, there have been innumerable wars, conflicts, and other destructive skirmishes, and nothing is so devastating to a country's economy. Further, recorded history has demonstrated that a surplus economy is absolutely necessary if humans are to have a high standard of education and leisure. Still further, the truism that times change slowly has been shown to be a proven fact considering the rate of change of traditions and mores in past civilizations (Brubacher, 1966, p. 76 et ff.).

There are at least several additional reasons why the advent of leisure may have been retarded. For example, many existing autocratic political systems continued to prevail, and it finally took revolutions to overthrow them before the concept of political democracy had an opportunity to grow. Additionally, the power of the Church—an almost absolute power—had to be weakened before the concept of separation of church and state could become a reality in the Western world. Finally, the beginnings of the natural sciences had to be consolidated into very real gains before advancing technology could lead Europe into the Industrial Revolution, the outcome of which we possibly still cannot foresee clearly. We do know that the opportunity for leisure—and for beneficial use of such time—was furthered because at least people's working hours were brought down to what seemed to be a relatively low figure.

We are continually being told that citizens in the industrialized world now have more leisure than ever before. Sweeping statements such as this need careful scrutiny in light of the changing conditions we are encountering. We also read, for example, that the population may be broken down into classes depending upon the number of hours people will be required to work. Some people, they said, will be paid not to work, a situation that those living in ghettos might both wryly and angrily agree to if questioned. One factor often omitted from studies about leisure is that a large number of family or "living" units now require two or three incomes to survive in the style to which they have become accustomed.

If indeed there is, generally speaking, a trend toward the provision of more leisure for the average person, we still should understand that the promotion of the concept of education for leisure depends a great deal on whether the prevailing educational philosophy will allow sufficient support for the inclusion of such programs in the formal educational system. The inclusion of such opportunities within adult education and community recreation programs is, of course, already an accepted fact—but more recently to a greater extent on a increasingly pay-as-you-go basis.

It is legitimate, then, to inquire about what people will do with any leisure thay may have achieved. Shortly we will review briefly what they have done with it in the past. But first there are a few other points to be made and a few definitions to consider. For example, shall such leisure be used for play, as typically conceived, or for what might be (correctly) called recreation education? (I say "correctly" here, because a few recreation leaders incorrectly—etymologically speaking—urged those who prepare recreation leaders to give the name "recreation education" to professional training for recreational leadership.) My objective here is to trace the use of leisure throughout history briefly, and then to analyze how it should be used according to the major philosophical trends in the Western world. Finally, major attention will be given to (1) physical recreation activities, although you should understand that necessarily the following four aspects (interests) within the total recreation picture are also extremely important: (2) social, (3) communicative, (4) aesthetic and creative, and (5) "learning" (or educational hobbies). Now let us take a brief excursion to review what people in earlier societies did when and if they had leisure away from daily toil.

Brief Historical Background

Early Societies. In primitive and preliterate societies, there probably was not so sharp a division between work and play as in civilized societies. Adults had a difficult time with basic survival activities and enjoyed very little leisure. Such leisure as a particular family or tribe was able to earn was probably used for play activity of an aimless nature, conjecturally quite similar to that of animals. Later, embryonic cultures developed certain folkways and ceremonials of a more controlled nature. Inclement weather, even in our own day a mighty influence, may at least have afforded some leisure time.

A division of labor—with resultant leisure for some—occurred in Egypt, Mesopotamia, China, and India, generally considered the first great civilizations of the world. These social developments came about through favorable environments and people's correct responses to certain environmental and social stimuli. The wealth accumulated through the toil of the masses was soon in the hands of a relatively few individuals. Historically, these fortunate few were the first to enjoy anything like an extended period of leisure. Some used this free time to speculate and learn more about their environment; others developed various arts and skills, or participated in sports. Still others squandered the time in seemingly meaningless pursuits.

In Egypt as one example, however, we find a great accumulation of formal knowledge made available because religious leaders acquired wealth and leisure. And so it was in early civilization that a type of culture developed because several ruling classes of people emerged in the stratification of society. It is to the credit of these early humans that any free time earned was used to discover, create, and/or invent early sculpture, music, pictorial art, dancing, religious ceremonies, medicine, language, and writing.

The Athenian Greeks. The Athenians developed a very high standard of living for ancient times. During their "golden age" they used their leisure most wisely. Although Athenian democracy is often acclaimed as an ideal, the existence of three social classes (freemen, non-citizens, and slaves) must not be overlooked. Education was confined to native freemen, and Athenian women were regarded as inferior creatures to be kept on a low intellectual plane.

Nevertheless, there were some extremely important developments at this point in humankind's history. Service to the state was not a new concept, but the idea of a many-sided education involving training of the mental, moral, physical, and aesthetic aspects of human nature is an ideal the world had not seen before and has not been able to realize since. Here for the first time, also, we see the beginning of the idea of a liberal education for a freeman and citizen, as opposed to the practical training of a noncitizen or slave. It was a broad, general education that promoted the harmonious, all-round development of the individual through an education that emphasized letters, literature and music, conduct, and gymnastic exercises and sport.

The Ancient Romans. The early Romans had not yet achieved enough of a surplus economy to have the free time needed for the pursuit of the liberal arts. In fact, it has been said that the Romans never did more than merely perpetuate the Greek ideal of liberal education anyhow. But whether they fully appreciated it is another question. Here again we find a stratification of society with the senators and the equites (equestrians) enjoying far greater wealth and social status than the plebeians. Once again there were the freemen who could vote, but there were as many as five million slaves toward the end of the republic in the territory now known as Italy. As usual, wealth determined leisure, and leisure determined the extent to which a person would be educated. Leisure was, in fact, synonymous with freedom.

How did the Romans use their leisure? Accumulated wealth led to unnecessary luxuries and selfish individualism. Social standing was determined to a large extent by the amount of one's personal fortune, and crass materialism became the leading philosophy of the time. Crime increased at all levels and often went unpunished. As the way of life changed, the formerly active Roman found himself unemployed and with no source of income. The state fed and entertained these people with great exhibitions, and soon a passion for the games and the circus grew. Many baths were provided for the physical and social recreation of the masses as well. Another strong factor in Rome's decline was the misuse of power by the senatorial class that resulted in a series of civil wars just before Augustus came into power. What once had been an extremely strong state disintegrated as the rich exploited the poor, civil freedoms gradually vanished, and moral fiber weakened.

The (Early) Middle Ages. In the period known as the Middle Ages, in Europe, the same social system existed, with minor variations. The ruling class had its own pattern of leisure and usually decided what the masses, the villagers and peasants, would be allowed to do. Whereas the knights did their jousting at tournaments, and the gentlemen engaged in hunting and hawking, fencing, dancing, gaming, and other such activities, the common folk had their fairs, dramas, celebrations, and festivals. Recreations were often carried to excess, and such activities were typically frowned upon by the third social class, the Church.

The Church glorified asceticism and hard labor. Leisure activities were generally condemned, as they tended to destroy godliness; the human spirit was exhorted to control the flesh and keep it from vices. Thus, any types of recreation gratifying the bodily senses were to be put aside because of the resulting harm to the individual seeking salvation. A total of eight weeks was typically set aside for a multitude of religious celebrations. These periods were specifically designed for purposes other than leisure pastimes. Such restrictions were difficult to enforce, however, no matter how many rules and regulations the Church laid down. We should not forget that leisure was still not something you earned; it was the property of one particular class in society.

The Renaissance. The Renaissance was the beginning of a most important time for modern people in the Western world. There were, of course, many influences that gradually brought about the change in attitude away from the narrow, "other-worldly" atmosphere that existed prior to this period. Intellectual advancement of a scientific nature had been taking place among non-Christians, a development the Christian world finally began to realize in the late 14th and 15th centuries. A number of humanists of this time made a strong effort to renew the earlier concept of "a sound mind in a sound body" (an adage carried over from Seneca, the Roman). This concept remains as an ideal still today—although an incorrect and insufficient one!—as the 2ist century begins. Vast economic changes were also occurring as commerce developed throughout the "developed" world of the time. The rise of free cities, the developing spirit of nationalism, and the growth of industry and banking all contributed to a new way of life.

The real meaning of the Renaissance and the centuries immediately following may well be found in the spirit of inquiry that developed, a type of scientific inquiry that swept aside many earlier dogmas. The founding of many universities contributed greatly to this spread of knowledge and learning, as did the development of paper and the printing press. The power of the Church declined somewhat, as attention shifted to the problems of individuals attempting to carve out early versions of "the good life" on Earth.

One may well ask why it took so long—so many thousands of years—before the possibility of earning and using leisure became a reality for the average person. This again is not a simple question to answer. For one thing, there have been innumerable wars, and these automatically destroy any surplus economy existing, a economic state that is absolutely necessary for a high standard of education and leisure. Second, the traditions and mores of a civilization change slowly and probably do so only under concerted intellectual, social, political, and economic pressure. It took revolutions to overthrow absolutist regimes before the concept of separation of church and state became a reality. Fourth, the beginnings of the natural sciences had to be consolidated into very real practical gains before advanced technology could lead us into an Industrial Revolution, the final outcome of which we still cannot foresee.

Further, not the least of these changes was the rebirth of so-called philosophical naturalism during the early days of the Renaissance. Actually, unrefined naturalism has been considered by some to be the oldest philosophy in the Western world, dating to about 500 years before Christ. Thales, who lived in Miletus in Asia Minor, believed he had found the final stuff of the universe within nature. He and his contemporaries saw an order in nature that was both logical and exemplary for people to follow. Both their intuition and their reason told them that we should allow nature to take its course. This early philosophy actually bore a close relationship to the later individual humanism of the twelfth and thirteenth centuries. The educational aim of humanism was the development of the individual personality through a liberal education, with the "humanities" replacing the "divinities." The world of nature should be studied; the real life of the past should be examined; and the joys of living should be extolled. Physical education, sport, and games were considered to be natural activities that should be encouraged.

Naturalism emerged in the 18th century as a full-blown philosophy of life with obvious educational implications. These implications were expressed magnificently by Jean Jacques Rousseau, who encouraged educators to study the child carefully and then to devise an educational plan based on this examination. The results of this approach became evident in the educational innovations of the next two centuries both in Europe and North America. For the first time, play was recognized by some as a factor of considerable importance in the development of the child. The aftermath of these new ideas has been of untold value to the field of health, physical education, recreation, sport, and dance.

North America. Before leisure could be used in North America, it had to be earned. Furthermore, certain prevailing ideas about idleness had to be broken down. Neither of these occurrences took place overnight. Recreational patterns have gradually emerged as the United States and Canada have grown and prospered. Initially, people originated their own recreational pursuits in an unorganized fashion. Following this, gradually all types of commercial recreational opportunities were made available, some of dubious value. And, finally, public and voluntary agencies were created to meet the many recreational needs and interests of the populace. These patterns of recreation are now proceeding concurrently as the 21st century begins, and careful analysis is most difficult.

From an economic standpoint it could be argued that we now find ourselves in a very favorable situation. The average work week has gradually been cut almost in half. However, steadily increasing inflation and the accompanying rise in the cost of living, not to mention the greater involvement of women in the workplace, have blurred the resultant picture considerably. Nevertheless, some people are now choosing leisure instead of more work, or early retirement because they want to enjoy life. Many others, because of changing employment patterns, are being forced to accept an increased amount of leisure, although they do not have all the material possessions of life they might wish to have.

From a historical standpoint, the Puritans presumably equated play with idleness, and hence evil, and tried to suppress it by legislation. At the same time the Virginians were enjoying a variety of recreational pursuits with relatively few twinges of conscience. The 18th century saw a marked change in recreational habits as some leisure was indeed earned. Such activities as dancing, hunting, fishing, horse racing, barn raisings, and all sorts of community enterprises characterized this period. After 1800 a transitional period set in, as sectionalism caused many different patterns of recreation to flourish. The steady movement toward urbanization gave commercialized recreation the opportunity to develop unrestrained; yet we might say that recreation as an organized structure of the democratic way of life was only in its infancy in the late 19th century.

Earning Leisure in North America. Before a considerable amount leisure became available in North America, however, it had to be earned. The land mass had to be actually conquered and mastered by the various settlers. When Jacques Cartier looked at Canada, for example, he is purported to have said, "This must be the land that God gave Cain!" ("Time Essay," 1967). It has been pointed out, also, that certain prevailing ideas about leisure had to be broken down (*Holiday*, 1956). From an economic standpoint, there is more to the question of leisure for the average person than that fact that some people had a lot of money, and that she or he had very little of the same commodity.

A more fundamental issue was that the level of production was not high enough to support the population at more than a subsistence level. The advent of industrial technology changed this imbalance to a considerable degree. Over the past 100 years, the average worker has produced more than five times as much as previously. Moreover, while the length of the work week was decreasing, the value of people's production was growing 25 times. Further, the population increase did not offset this development. So, by the mid-1960s, the average work week during this period had been cut almost in half. At that point many people were choosing leisure instead of more work, because they wanted to "enjoy life." And many others were being forced to accept an increased amount of leisure, although they didn't have all of the material possessions that they wanted (Michael, 1961, pp. 14-24). The question being asked at that time was, "Will the people—the taxpayers—make sufficient funding available so that 'education for leisure' can actually become part of the overall program offered by most schools?"

By the close of the 20th century, therefore, an era characterized by the greatest surplus economy the "developed" world had ever seen, we had witnessed a vast new development that may be called organized recreation. The outlines of this pattern had been barely discernible toward the end of the 19th century, but in the 20th century the development of public and voluntary agency recreation in the United States and Canada was absolutely phenomenal. Further social and economic changes had taken place; professional associations had developed; professional preparation for recreational leadership had mushroomed at both the undergraduate and graduate levels; and city-supported recreation programs along with community centers in schools formed a network across the United States and Canada.

A Unique Phenomenon Occurs. The degree to which taxpayers will ever want an education-for-leisure entity within the educational program—or will not do so—is the one large question to be answered. Indeed, whether it would be supported financially, even if it were wanted, is an even larger question. However, it is true that, along with a steadily growing economy, we have witnessed in both the United States and Canada, the occurrence of a unique phenomenon in world history—an organized pattern of community recreation embodying a wide variety of cultural opportunities. As stated above, the outline of this pattern had been barely discernible toward the end of the nineteenth century, but in the last half of the twentieth century the development of public and voluntary agency recreation has been absolutely phenomenal. (The unbridled growth of commercial recreation is another serious question, but it will not be discussed here.) As further social and economic changes have taken place, professional associations have developed, professional preparation for recreational leadership has mushroomed, and municipally supported recreation and parks programs, along with community centers, for an intricate network across the United States and Canada.

Advancing industrial civilization has brought this truly significant advantage to the people, but it has created many problems as well. One of these that impinges indirectly on the use of leisure is that of increasing specialization of function—that is, some people manage and other people labor. This has resulted in an uneven distribution of wealth. Of course, there has always been specialization of function of one sort or another in societies, and the leaders have invariably ended up with the lion's share of the "good things" of life. The people with more money have been able as a result to afford longer periods and different types of education and recreation for themselves and their children. Of course, the labor movement has been striving mightily since its inception to reverse this trend to a reasonable degree. However, organized labor has encountered significant intransigence recently on the part of both government and business, much of this occasioned by governmental debt and rather general business downsizing. These developments impact inevitably on both the educational structure and the recreational opportunities available within society. This struggle for both educational and recreational services is crucial to the advancement of the social welfare-state concept, an ideology that has been popular with both the middle and lower classes.

10. HUMAN MORALITY IS NOT DISINTEGRATING

Up to this point, much of what has been said above has been challenging and yet often disheartening too. So much of what has been said and done, both in our history generally and in this discussion specifically, relates to the question of both individual and social values. This is a vital question actually, because the answer to it relates so directly to what people do with their leisure.

However, if we ever hope to find agreement on the question as to whether people should have (or may have) free time and what they should do (or not do) with it, we must indeed reach much greater consensus on the matter of values, ethics, and morality. One of the more serious problems or issues upon which greater consensus is needed in this connection is that of human morality and ethics. This issue arose starkly starting in the late 1960s, and is still a topic of great concern in the late 1990s. *The New York Times* reported, for example, that "our morality is disintegrating because its foundation is eroding." *The Washington Post* asserted that "the core of U.S. national character has been damaged because we've lost our sense of virtue!"

Despite these assertions I believe that human morality is not disintegrating. For example, although denying a person's right to choose abortion is still being argued vigorously and vociferously by a minority in the United States, the question of gays in the military has been only temporarily resolved. Also, we are still finding difficulty in granting full rights as citizens to same-sex alliances. Yet it seems reasonable to me that, if a person is willing to die for his or her country in military service, how this person fulfills sexual desires in the privacy of a bedroom should hardly be a major issue today. Nevertheless, the question of immorality and its relationship to the legal system is still with us and won't go away easily.

An Evolving Value System. The evidence indicates that we will continue to be confronted with an assortment of problems that revolve about the value system of our North American culture. The Cold War with the former U.S.S.R. is over, but we are still faced with a continuation of a "hot" Culture War on this continent. To be sure, this appears to be somewhat more of a problem in the United States, but Canada will inevitably be drawn more fully into the ongoing controversy as the increasing impact of its "ethnic-diversity" approach sinks in. Also, those who plead for more "Canadian-content" in Canadian culture can hardly prevail totally because of the daily media blitz from the south.

The philosopher, John Kekes (1987), calls the argument that "the world is going to Hell in a handbasket," morally speaking, The Disintegration Thesis. This position is as follows:

1. the value system of the culture no longer offers significant rationale for subordinating one's self to the common good;

2. a healthy democratic government depends on values that come from religion (the Judeo-Christian tradition, that is, [to this point]);

3. human rights are based on the moral worth that a loving God has granted to each human soul; and

4. authority in social affairs is empowered because of underlying transcendent moral law (Brookings Institution).

What this all adds up to is that the "disintegration thesis" holds that society's basic problem is moral.

What rebuttal may be offered to the idea that our culture is sliding down a slippery slope to moral bankruptcy? Kekes argues that the issue is simply this: Moral change has been confused with moral disintegration. He agrees that are many seemingly disturbing moral issues today, but he then inquires about the significance of these facts as a "new morality" struggles to be born. Basically what is being abandoned, he claims, is the idea that there is one and only one set of virtues for a human life, one **Summum Bonum** (to place the dilemma in terms of Latin nomenclature).

The opposite viewpoint to The Disintegration Thesis is that a gradual change in our morality has indeed been occurring, and that such change will continue. However, in this change from a single morality to a pluralistic one in North America, there are still many good traits or virtues present in our daily lives. We still have the basic concepts of freedom, knowledge, happiness, justice, love, order, privacy, wisdom, etc. with which to guide and develop our personal lives and social living. However, we need to understand that in this ever-increasing pluralistic culture none of these concepts is necessarily reducible to the other—and especially not to the idea that there is one transcendental moral law.

This means that each person should work in his or her life for some reasonable or acceptable combination of such values as love, freedom, justice, etc. This sounds great, and it may be all well and good to those individuals ready to accept the changes toward a pluralistic morality that are occurring. But to the defenders of The Disintegration Thesis, the argument for acceptance of this developing situation simply adds fuel to their fire.

To the one-morality group, any individually selected amalgam of values and virtues represents just one more symptom of the moral bankruptcy that is taking place right before our eyes. So, if the advocates of a new, more pluralistic morality hope to win their argument, they must show that there is sufficient continuity between the old and the new, between monistic and pluralistic morality.

How can we move an analysis of this issue one step further along? One way to do this, according to Kekes, is to look for regularity and continuity in morality from one historical period to another. What we have been doing is to become too concerned about the seeming irregularity and discontinuity as North American culture changes from monism to pluralism in ethics and morality. (In my *Who knows what's right anymore?: A guide to personal decision-making* [Victoria, BC, Canada. Trafford, 2002], I offer an initial three-step approach that can even be of help interculturally in the making of ethical decisions. [See www.earlezeigler.com and click on Trafford on the home page.])

Disproving the Disintegration Thesis. However, the only way that we can disprove the Disintegration Thesis is to show that human nature still exhibits a deeper, powerful, more important continuity in moral affairs than appears through initial analysis of the seeming confusion that confronts us today. In approaching this rebuttal, the purpose of morality should be examined first. Let us argue, for example, that its aim is to increase good and to decrease evil in human affairs. As we strive to do this, we should understand, of course, that some goods and some evils are the result of natural forces in the world. However, many others goods and evils are the result of human action or inaction. For example, some individual and/or group is responsible for the evil inherent in the infamous Oklahoma City tragedy or in the World Trade Center disaster. Conversely, think of all the good that has resulted from this as literally thousands of people made almost superhuman efforts to restore people's lives in those truly tragic situations to some state of normalcy.

Further, in our effort to improve the state of morality, we can recognize and then understand that there are many similarities among the various world's cultures on the subject of goods and evils. Nevertheless, we can't escape the fact that there are also many individual, social, cultural, and historical differences on the subject of morality. However, despite all of these differences between and among cultures, it is humanity itself that necessarily establishes the continuity and regularity between our earlier monistic morality and the pluralistic morality in which direction many of the world's peoples are moving inevitably and inescapably!

And so, it is maintained by Kekes, it is this very unchangeable continuity that places boundaries on, and thereby limits, the scope of moral change and the very kinds of moral conflicts that we are confronting today. How may we define this continuity? Kekes defines it simply as that group of "universally human, culturally invariant, and historically constant characteristics" that every creature living in a social environment in the world possesses. Here I am referring to (1) physiological capacities and needs, and (2) psychological capacities and similarities. The evidence for this comes from both the natural sciences and the social sciences—that is, from physiology on the one hand, and from psychology and sociology on the other.

These needs, capacities, and similarities include (1) facts about the body and the self, (2) facts about close relationships, and (3) facts about social living. Note in this connection, also, the strong similarity with Maslow's hierarchy of fundamental propositions about human nature. He theorized that we move from up the scale from survival (the instinct to satisfy physiological, safety, and personal needs and interests) to commergence (from belonging to conformity to affection) to differentiation (growing concern with status, power, respect) to self-development (fulfilling drives toward learning, creativity, and love).

You may ask, "How does all of this relate to the morality issue?" The answer is this: the fact that we all have this universal and unchanging human nature is morally important. Why? Because it gives us insight into what actions or inactions in life count as beneficial or harmful to our human nature. These universally good and evil things are, respectively,

1. the satisfaction of needs and interests by exercising our capacities
and

2. the accompanying frustration and injury that will result if these universal needs and interests are not met.

What this all adds up to, therefore, is a re-assessment of the goods necessary for the continuity of human nature for which we all strive. These universal human goods that should be maintained and preserved in our increasingly pluralistic morality underlie the premise that human life is better if it possesses these goods in abundance and worse if evils abound to decrease the presence of these avowed goods.

This position offered by Kekes finally "asserts" that human morality is not disintegrating. Viewed in this way, the central task of morality is not to worry about the peripheral aspects of the increasingly pluralistic morality. It is to foster conditions that bring about conditions that raise the levels of the core aspects of human nature—that is, self-direction, intimacy, and decency. If we understand this, and agree to it, this takes us part of the way—not all of it!—toward the resolution of the puzzling ethics and morality question plaguing our culture at the present.

11. RECREATIONAL ACTIVITIES SHOULD EMBODY TRULY VALUABLE EXPERIENCES FOR ALL

Moving from a discussion of present morality and ethics, an explanation that offers a highly desirable "moral environment" as we seek ways to achieve "the (almost mythical) good life," I am suggesting here that through involvement in the finest types of recreational activities we can take a giant step in this direction. I say this because, whether we travel, sing a song, turn on television or radio, surf the Internet, take a walk, weed the garden, go for a swim, write a poem, go fishing, read a book, attend a discussion group, sketch a landscape, knit socks in a rocker, or climb a mountain, we are engaging in a form or level of recreational activity.

And yet still today there are many people who refuse to recognize that opportunities for recreational participation and recreation education should have a place of permanence in our communities. Many of these people seem to have a lack of a leisure philosophy. Perhaps they have had to work so hard along the way that the development of such a philosophy about leisure has not been possible. With these folks, one is reminded of the very early days on the continent when all people struggled with a bare subsistence economy.

Yet, others have been understandably forced to such a position more recently by the frequent need for two wage earners in a family to make enough money to get by. Where there is only one person gainfully employed in a family, the situation is often even worse. Finally, many simply can't find employment and, for one or more reasons, are on welfare or workfare.

How Good Is the Life We Have Created?

So I ask you: take a candid look at our civilization from the standpoint of human values. How good, in human terms, is this life that we have created? What has been lost, and what has been gained, since the human has given up making products with his hands to make them by machine—or to have them made for him by robots? And where do we go from here? Can we create a society where ever more people will find happiness and fulfillment despite the fact that more and more of them are crowded together in heavily populated cities? Or will things get continually worse because of continuing population growth and poor "husbandry" of the earth.

At this point we should define the term "value." For purposes of discussion, I have followed the pragmatic definition of value here: a value is that which has proved to be useful through experience. Following from this, in an effort to make the case for the presence of human values in recreation and leisure, we need to determine what all types of recreational pursuits have been able to offer of a useful nature to people.

As we know, there are many types of recreation recommended to us. In North America, we appreciate that recreation, whether it be "taken" spontaneously, commercially, or as a choice in a community-based program organized for the citizens' benefit, should be available to all people, everywhere. I now believe that recreation should be conceived as an aspect of daily living. I accept this because we are finding that humans have a basic need for it as they search endlessly for a full, happy life.

But what is happiness? Is it the "natural effect" of a good life. And, if we are ever able to decide what "the good life" is in a democratic society—generally speaking, that is—could we dare to make a guess when such would be available to all people on the North American continent? In the whole world? And, if so, what sort of a prospect will we face? Paradoxically, making privileges available to all that are now only available to a relatively few, "well-to-do" people may afford us all a type of life that we never anticipated. It may well develop that, if an effort is made to grant all privileges to all people, the impossibility of such an arrangement will soon become apparent. (Someone guessed recently that it would take 3 and 1/2 earths "resource-wise" to bring everyone on earth up to "modern" standards.) Perhaps the only hope for such a possiblity to become a reality at some distant future point is for absolutely everything to be completely automated.

If this were to come about, however—if the work week gets shorter and shorter as certain pundits were predicting earlier—there will be even fewer people to keep the wheels turning daily. Who will want to perform the million and one tasks necessary to keep the society functioning? Who will mind the store, repair the plumbing, clean up the garbage, put heels on children's battered shoes, and even want the stress of teaching school, coaching sport teams, and leading children in non-competitive recreational activities. Will you (my reader) do it, if—for example—many people are being paid by the government not to work?

Will We Ever Have Four Different Leisure Classes?

Paid not to work; how might that happen? I recall a theory involving cybernetics proposed by Michael back in 1962. We were told that cybernation, with its automation and sophisticated computer technology, would eventually bring additional leisure to practically all people on this continent. However, he added that to this point we recognize but dimly the problems that will be created. Presumably there would be a transitional stage that would extend over several decades before a relatively stable future state sets in. In planning for the transitional period, Michael (pp. 29-33). postulated four different leisure classes as follows:

1. Leisure Class One—the unemployed.
2. Leisure Class Two—the low-salaried, unskilled employeees working short hours.
3. Leisure Class Three—the adequately paid to high-salaried group working short hours.
4. Leisure Class Four—those with no more leisure than they have now (i.e., very few hours of leisure indeed)

Of course the interesting thing about such development purportedly on the horizon is that we don't have to cybernate. As Michael explained, "Cybernation is by nature that sort of process that will be introduced selectively by organization, industry, and locality" (p. 28). It could actually "sneak up" on a community, and most people would not even recognize it. And, presumably, if its effects are too harsh, it would always be theoretically possible to "decybernate." To sum up at this point, it appears that some future Shakespeare may well say, "To cybernate, or not to cybernate, that is the question!" My disclaimer at this point is simply that the mood of this culture today would never permit decybernation to take place.

RECREATION EDUCATION TRIANGLE

Four Levels of Participation

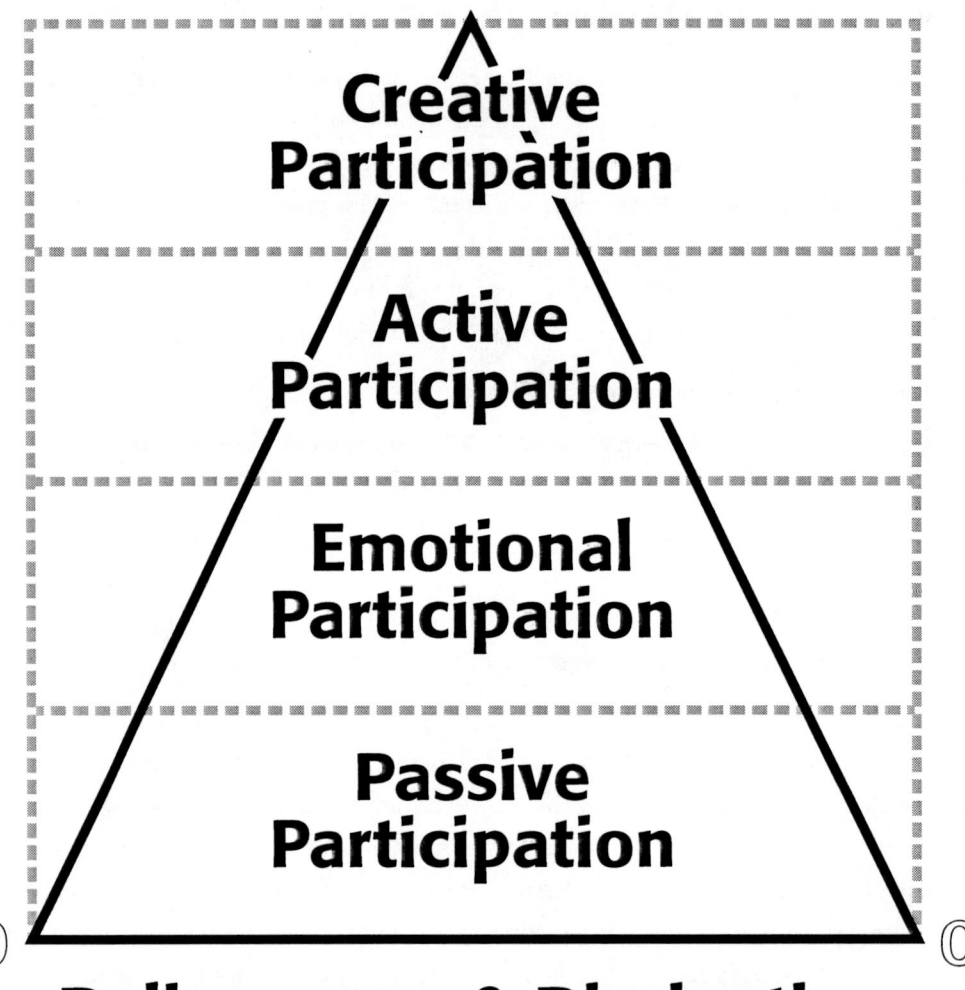

Creative Participation

Active Participation

Emotional Participation

Passive Participation

Delinquency & Dissipation

FIGURE 1

For the sake of argument, let us say that it gradually becomes possible for most people to increasingly have more free time. What would they do with this extra time away from work at some future time in this culture? Would they simply do more of what many people are actually doing with their leisure today? Have conditions changed from the situation described at mid-century? J.B. Nash (1953), one of the leading recreation philosophers of this mid-century period, stated that people were doing four types of things with it. They were either:

1. going to sleep mentally in a "looking on" process; (i.e., "passive participation" or "spectatoritis"),

2. getting involved somewhat more (i.e., "emotional participation"),

3. getting involved actively (i.e., "active participation"), or

4. engaging in some qualitative phase of creative participating activity (i.e., "creative participation")

If we consider that these types of involvement are "positive," to a greater or lesser degree, Nash explained further that people were often wasting time negatively in delinquency or dissipation. (See Figure 1 above)

With his assessment, Nash was simply explaining his belief that the advanced nations are facing the awesome spectacle of a considerable segment of the world degenerating because of the inventiveness of humans. For this reason we can argue that communities should be testing the recreational "literacy" of their citizens. Obviously, it is too ambitious to have as an ultimate aim the involvement of 100 percent of the people in some phase of the community recreation program. There are undoubtedly some people who have no need for activity within an organized program. If we are to be even the least bit scientific, we should determine what recreational skills and experience people have had and at what level of involvement. The aim should be to make sound, wholesome, creative recreation a significant part of the lives of all people.

The breadth of any community's recreation program may be portrayed as a revolving wheel with five spokes, the space between the spokes being the five categories of possible recreational involvement: (1) physical recreational interests, (2) social recreational interests, (3) communicative recreational interests, (4) esthetic and creative recreational interests, and (5) "learning" recreational interests (i.e., hobbies, etc.). (See Figure 2 below.)

Recreation Education's Revolving Wheel

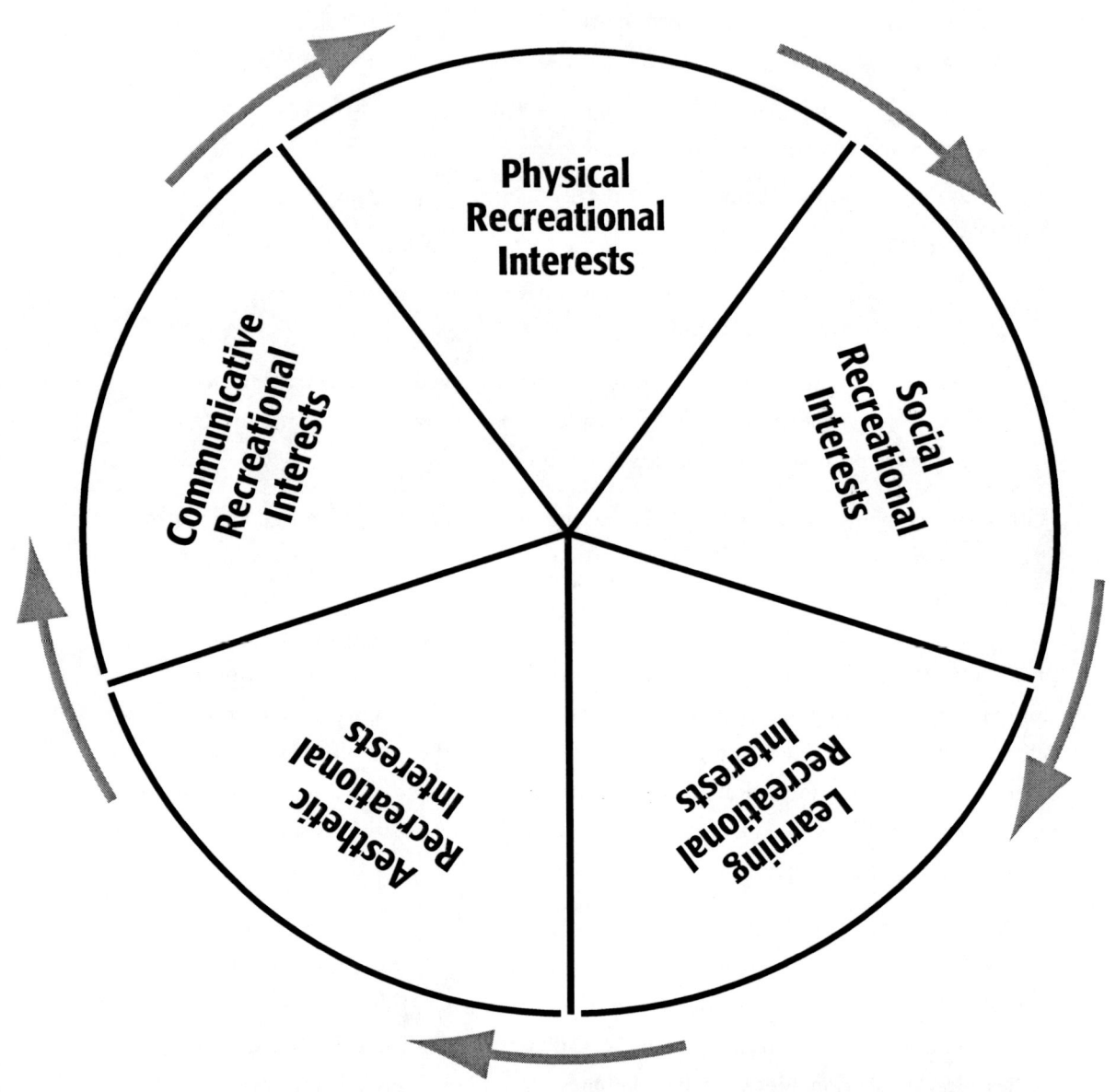

FIGURE 2

Thus, the "revolving wheel" of a community's recreational program is rotating before us at all times—if, and only if, the services of a well-planned program are made available. As individuals we are in the enviable position of a person with the option of "throwing darts at a revolving wheel." The choices are ours to make. We probably can't hope to have people participating creatively in all five area of recreational interest. There is simply not enough time available at present if a person must work for a living. From a health standpoint, we should strive to interest people in some form of healthful recreational activity of a physical nature. Wholesome social recreational interests make a strong contribution to mental health, also. We should at least have an understanding and appreciation of the other areas through "participation" at the "passive" and "emotional" or vicarious levels. The argument here, then, is that there is more human value in recreation as a person participates at the higher levels of each of the five categories of recreational interest. And, as stated above, an examination of history soon clarifies that no higher civilization has survived for long when the people had an abundance of leisure. If the dream of abundant leisure does become realized, we should plan now to educate people recreationally (so to speak). We definitely do not want in the far-distant future to see the possibility realized that an anonymous poet warned us about:

> Science, it seems, is now well on the way
> To achieve its considerate aims for us;
>
> First, machines to provide us with leisure to play;
> Then machines to play various games for us.
>
> When machines do our work and machines do our play,
> We'll rejoice, for we'll then be in clover.
>
> We'll have nothing to do all the livelong day—
> Till machines that do nothing take over.

Returning to reality, however, as the world moves along in the 21st century we are a far cry from a civilization where "we have nothing to do all the livelong day!" The world is nowhere near to the sort of utopia envisioned above in the rhyme. In fact, we are finding a widening gap between the "haves" and the "have-nots." And yet even many of those who "have" are in danger of realizing that this wonderful dream of leisure is not quite what they expected. To avoid this disappointment, the late J.B. Nash was farsighted enough also to urge us to form a new concept of the term "play."

First, he felt this was necessary because of its tremendous educational implications for the future of our way of life. Second, we should do this because even today there are still so many carry-overs regarding the idea of play as a "harum-scarum, do-nothing activity" that lacks any disciplinary qualities. This translates into a narrow-minded idea that play is merely a time-consuming but joyous activity that children take part in at avery opportunity. A progression from this belief might be that recreation, however characterized, is for more mature adults.

Which Kinds of Play & Recreation Can Be Useful to People?

Any further delineation of the possible differences between play and recreation necessarily returns us to the idea of "human values." We would do well to ask ourselves a basic question: which kinds of play and recreation are useful to people in their lives? It has become imperative that we do this, that we carry out such evaluation. When you get right down to it, this makes sense. No program of recreation, or education for that matter, is worth its salt that does not regularly test and measure and then evaluate its progress. How does the field of recreation, for example, measure its progress? Does greater numbers of participants mean anything? It might, but not unless we know what the people are doing.

Does a larger budget mean that the recreation director is successful? Once again, it might, but it might also mean that he or she is lulling the city council into acquiescence by inadequate types of activities that are making the proverbial turnstiles click. All of this means, therefore, that we should ask questions about the recreation programs provided, about the activities people (i.e., you, me, our children, our friends) are engaging in spontaneously, and about the activities the masses are paying for commercially.

On the home front we watch the surges and declines of the economy apprehensively as companies large and small experiment with mergers, downsizing, and "becoming creative" with accounts and balances. The computer revolution is in full swing, and what this means to the traditional job market is anybody's guess. We understand that the level of automation is steadily increasing, and that many people are being displaced in regard to job security and future aspirations. Politicians are talking about workfare—and implementing it in some cases! Yet they can't seem to find either employment for people forced out of work or sufficient support for the allocation of funds for them to be retrained.

In such a situation, the provision of low-paying, bare-subsistence jobs in service industries is not going to be the answer. In addition to improved competency training for the many new types and categories of positions that are becoming available, education for leisure also demands serious consideration. If people are working, they need free time for "re-creation." If they are not working, the need for worthwhile and creative use of leisure—including re-training—is even more important. Situations that provide passive and even "vicarious" recreational opportunities will not be sufficient. Active and creative recreational experiences are required to give life added zest and purpose. And we dare not forget: history shows that no civilization has survived for long when the people had too much free time.

Viewed in this light, Sullivan as long ago as 1967 spoke to "The challenge of the city." The basic question then was, "Can we continue our unprecedented development on a continent where most people will find happiness and satisfaction?" The strength of such a question becomes even more stark today as we steadily increase the population of the many cities and suburbs resulting in further urban sprawl and the attendant problems that such overcrowding brings. How differently, if at all, would such a question be phrased today?

Such inquiry is especially important if people's work is not challenging. If such is the case, and it very often does lack in challenge, men and women of all ages will look to their leisure to provide them with excitement, adventure, and the opportunity to grow and develop. Let's face it: involvement in movement activities is one important characteristic that distinguishes people from rocks on the ground. When a person goes into decline and ceases to be active, death often follows closely behind. Thus we must be certain that people in today's world have frequent opportunities to acquire enhanced human values through their involvement in recreational pursuits at the active and creative levels.

Recommended Approaches for Improving Life's Quality

Csikszentmihalyi (1993), seeking to help humans "free themselves of the dead hand of the past," has proposed selected "approaches to life that will improve its quality and lead to joyful involvement." However, he stresses that humans are now confronted with a "memes versus genes" dilemma. "Meme" is the term introduced in the 1970s by the British biologist, Richard Dawkins, who coined the noun from the Greek term mimesis to describe a set of "cultural instructions" passed on by example from one generation to another. A gene is, of course, the basic physical unit of heredity about which we are hearing increasingly.

Csikszentmihalyi is fearful that humans' previous "adaptive successes"—the very ones that have helped people survive to the present—need to be re-assessed in the light of present conditions lest they destroy our future. He is referring here to (1) the organization of the brain, (2) the emergence of a primitive self, (3) the genetic instructions that helped us survive through past milennia, and (4) the competition with other people that is the result of the selective forces on which evolution is based. In addition, he is also concerned about a further danger—"the threat of the artifacts we have created to make our lives more comfortable" (p. 119). The problem here is that these "permanent patterns of matter or information produced by an act of human intentionality" (p. 120), although new on the humans' evolutionary stage, can over time assume lives of their own, so to speak. For example, the results of a few "mimetic parasites," such as the mind-altering drugs, alcohol and tobacco, have been literally devastating to a number of societies (or segments thereof).

Arguing that our unique heritage "brings with it an awesome responsibility" because we are at the cutting edge of evolution, he affirms that now we "can either direct our life energy toward achieving growth and harmony or waste the potentials we have inherited, adding to the sway of chaos and destruction" (pp. 3-4). Basically, Csikszentmihalyi is searching for ways that could "integrate the growth and liberation of the self with that of society as a whole" (p. 5). Essentially, he is recommending that we diligently seek what he calls "flow experiences" which are characterized by,

1. clear goals with instant feedback;

2. opportunities for acting decisively in situations where personal skills are suited to given challenges;

3. actions taken merging with awareness to facilitate concentration;

4. resulting concentration on the task at hand such that there is complete psycho-physical involvement;

5. a sense of potential control prevailing;

6. a loss of self-consciousness involving transcendence of ego boundaries occurring as the person experiences a sense of growth and of being part of some greater entity;

7. a sense of time altered so as to seem to pass faster; and

8. an experience that becomes autotelic, and thus creating the feeling that it is worth doing for its own sake (pp. 178-179).

He theorizes further that, even though intense flow experiences are relatively rare in everyday life, such experiences should indeed be increasingly possible in the play, work, study, or religious ritual of humans, **IF AND ONLY IF** the conditions outlined above are present.

Zeldin (1994), in his highly interesting An intimate history of humanity, both complements and supplements the work of Csikszentmihalyi by offering what he calls a "new vision of the past." He urges humankind to revisit the various individual feelings and personal relationships evidenced throughout history. In the process he recommends that individuals "form a fresh view both of their own personal history and of humanity's whole record of cruelty, misunderstanding, and joy" (p. vii). This revised vision of the past can be gradually achieved as the 21st century develops, Zeldin affirms—agreeing with Csikszentmihalyi—by deliberate efforts to reverse, through considered re-examination now and in the future, the unpleasant and unrewarding experiences of distant past generations. Because of this urgent need to remove the past's "dead hand," Zeldin is telling us starkly and simply that "those who don't learn from past experiences are doomed to repeat them!"

What Zeldin is affirming, also, is today's urgent need to:

1. help people revive their hopes,

2. search for their roots,

3. acquire immunity to loneliness,

4. invent new forms of love,

5. give respect instead of seeking power,

6. learn how to serve as intermediaries between people,

7. free themselves from fears,

8. develop rewarding friendships,

9. survive today's nuclear family crisis, and

10. choose a purposeful way of life, to name some of the ways in which we can turn future achievement of now often hidden aspirations into "flow experiences."

Interestingly, Lenk (1994), writing from a social-philosophical perspective, also envisions the need for "value changes" in the "achieving society." He asks the question, "Is life more about work or more about pleasure?" In response he suggests that societal conditions may increasingly be such that people will require additional opportunities for "creative achievement and active involvement." Proceeding from an "achievement theme" he developed previously, Lenk affirms that "we are in need of a new positive 'culture' of achievement and a humanised creative achievement principle" (pp. 92-93).

12. PHILOSOPHICAL ANALYSIS

It is a truism to state that many people are facing the twenty-first century with a good deal of fear. Behind us are all sorts of wars, depressions, and example of human's (mostly man's!) inhumanity to others, and yet there is much that gives hope for the future. The big "Hot Wars" are over for the present—not counting an ongoing struggle against terrorists—and the "Cold War" that could have led to a global war is now a thing of the past. This latter struggle could have spelled utter devastation for humankind, and fortunately now efforts toward nuclear disarmament have made significant progress. (The withdrawal of the U.S. from a longstanding ballistic missile treaty with Russia is a concern, of course, as is the ongoing conflict between India and Pakistan.) So now we try to comprehend the so-called peaceful and the actual shooting revolutions going on all about us. One primary task is to make certain that the power of nuclear destruction doesn't get in the hands of irresponsible governments, groups, orindividuals.

At present people all over view the coming and goings of the world's peoples through different sets of "lenses." Modern Europe is now, for example, that part of the Western world where humans began to reconceive the nature and place of the individual. What is now known as the (unrefined) philosophy of naturalism had its rebirth in the classical humanism of the early Renaissance. Unrefined naturalism has been considered by some to be the oldest philosophy in the Western world dating back to five hundred years B.C.E. Thales, who lived in Miletus in Asia Minor, believed that he had found the final substance of the universe within nature.

For these reasons, as well as others mentioned above, naturalism emerged in the eighteen century as a full-blown philosophy of life with obvious educational implications. These ideas were expressed magnificently by Jean Jacques Rousseau in the classic Emile in which he encouraged educators to study the child carefully and then to devise an educational plan based on this examination. The result of this approach became evident in the educational innovations of the next two centuries both in Europe and North America, not to mention certain other regions of the world. Thus, as a result, play was recognized by some for the first time as a factor of considerable importance in the child's development. The aftermath of these new ideas has been of untold value to the allied professions of health, physical education, sport, recreation, and dance.

Later thought (e.g., by Herbert Spencer in the mid-nineteenth century) discarded the original materialistic idea of Thales for the idea that energy was indeed the fundamental "substance" of the universe. The basic premise still prevailed, however, one which that nature exhibited order and that this order could be relied upon by humans. Thus, humans should be able to live simply and in harmony with nature with people's intuition and reason telling them that nature should be permitted to take its course.

The educational aims of naturalism within humanism included development of the individual personality through a liberal education based on classicial literature and art. The "humanities" were to replace the "divinities" in this theory. The belief was that the world of nature should be studied; the real life of the past should be examined; and the joys of living should be extolled. Within this approach, physical education and playful sport were considered to be natural activities that should be encouraged.

Values and Leisure Today

Depending on various backgrounds with many different orientations, including conflicting ideologies, philosophies, and religions, people are looking ahead idealistically, realistically, pragmatically, existentially, agnostically, atheistically, "communistically," "nihilistically," analytically, or what have you (Zeigler, 1989). This means that people view the subject of human values in a great varieties of ways.

There is no doubt but that what Toffler called "future shock" has already touched us. In many cases it has brought on a wave of nostalgia for the "good old times" when people felt more secure. I believe that we must battle against the idea of a return to the past. Such an opportunity will never present itself and, if it somehow did, people would find that they weren't ready to move in that direction anyhow. I have concluded that the basic problem of the present is not so much a question of the impossibility of the prevailing situation. Rather I view it as a question of confronting and coping with the complexities of modern living that people can achieve only if they rediscover their confidence.

Such an affirmation would embody a philosophic position known as "positive meliorism," a stance that affirms that society has within itself a tendency to improve. Accordingly, people should learn to drive themselves assiduously to bring about a steadily improving social situation (Durant, W. & Durant, A., 1968, p. 102). As I see it, such a personal philosophy makes much more sense that assuming either a stance of hardened pessimism or one of blind optimism.

Human Nature Viewed Historically

How one looks upon the surrounding world tends to lead our discussion to a consideration of human nature from a historical standpoint. Van Cleve Morris, in the mid-1950s, described the human by creating the following chronological series of definitions:

1. a rational animal,

2. a spiritual being,

3. a reservoir of knowledge,

4. a mind that can be trained, and

5. a problem-solving organism (1956).

Within this well-delineated conception, I personally envision the task of my physical education and sport profession as providing service to this "problem-solving organism" by helping it to cope effectively and efficiently with the many daily activities we face in sport, exercise, expressive movement, and play. Well conceived, such an experience should be part and parcel of every human's socialization in this evolving world (Zeigler, 1975, p. 405).

In 1964, Berelson and Steiner traced six historical views or image of the nature of the human being, in this case from the standpoint of behavioral science. The first view, designated as **the philosophic image,** pictured the ancient human as a person who uses reason to delineate the virtues. This was followed by the second view **the Christian image,** in which humans were "born in sin," but could redeem themselves through the transfiguring love of God if they could control their impulses leading to sin. The third view was developed during the Renaissance and was called **the political image**. This described one who achieved power through the exercise of will and thereby was able to take control of his or her social environment. In this way the required energy was brought to bear on the social scene resulting in the promotion of various religious and social ideologies.

During the 18th and 19th centuries, there gradually emerged a fourth view that was called **the economic image** of the human being. This image demonstrated the rationale behind the development of people who understood the essentials required in life to be financially successful. This human image was also coupled with political savoir faire. At the start of the 20th century, a fifth view. **the psychoanalytic image** was postulated, a view that envisioned a new form of love: self-love. Here it was necessary to understand the role that childhood experience played in the future development of the adult life. Also, there was an attempt to understand the subsequent influence of powerful sexual influences at work in early life experience, as well as that of certain significant developmental experiences that might have been repressed. Finally, Berelson and Steiner were able, because of the rapid growth of the behavioral sciences in the 20th century, to designate a sixth view that they called **the behavioral science image of man and woman**. This view described the human as a creature who was unceasingly adapting reality to his or her own ends. In this way the individual sought to make present reality more pleasant, more convenient, and more fruitful as society struggled on inexorably.

As we move along now in the 21st century, we need to give some thought as to whether a seventh view (?) of the human being is needed or desirable. Offhand it would appear to be difficult to improve upon the behavioral science image. Perhaps it will be just a question of modifying it, or even delineating it further. What attitude or stance should a person seek to acquire, or to achieve, in regard to work, use of leisure, political action, or other aspects of living and consumption? There are scholarly authors, Reid and Mannell (1990, pp. 9-10), for example, who believe that education for leisure should play a unique role in generation education.

Defining the "Good Life" (Kateb)

This book's title asks the question: "What Happened to the Good Life?" We can get some insight into answering this query by reviewing the proposals concerning the question of human "image" or "attitude" from a discussion offered by Kateb (1965) at the time when it was thought that the "new age of leisure" was just around the corner for Mr. and Mrs. Everyman/Everywoman. Proceeding carefully from what might be called a scholarly excursion into anthropological philosophy, Kateb offered for consideration the following progression of six possibilities or definitions on the subject of what constituted "the good life":

1. Laissez faire (or do what you want to do);

2. Maximimum of pleasure (whether physical, intellectual or whatever;

3. Play (keeping in mind that there are many definitions of this term in an unabridged dictionary);

4. Craft (pursuing one's interest in craft);

5. Political action (working to improve the social condition through political involvement); and

6. The life of the mind (using one's intellectual abilities).

Kateb's conclusion (or selection) was not surprising, considering that he was a college professor. He felt that the "life of the mind" offered humans the best possibility in the world today—and in the future. "Man," he concluded, with his mental faculties developed to their peak of perfection, "is the model for utopia, and this possiblity already exists in reality" (p. 472).

So, as I see it, in a democratic society men and women today should strive to be fully able and ready to choose one of the avenues available for the good life in keeping with their various talents and wishes. Accordingly, they will then be in a position, also, to bring the theories of either Morris, or Berelson and Steiner, or Kateb to bear as they make their respective decisions about this vital question.

As I view this matter personally, I have long since envisioned myself as a problem-solving organism (Morris), but I also see myself combining this approach with the behavioral science image concept (Berelson & Steiner) that involves adapting reality to my personal and social goals to the greatest possible extent. From the standpoint of even more personal reflection, I see no need to choose one or the other of Kateb's approaches to the detriment of any other. I believe that each approach has—to a degree—a place in a full and complete life in our culture. Also, I feel I would enlarge upon Kateb's possibilities keeping one additional thought in mind: I believe that the evidence is now there to justify the argument that the good life is one in which a human has the opportunity to live life more fully and longer through regular involvement in the finest type of developmental physical activity (vivre son corps), activity that is carried out with a full awareness of the science of ecology (an "ecological awareness").

Meaning and Significance

As we progress in a new century, we do so with hope and anticipation, but also with a good deal of apprehension. Behind us are all sorts of wars, depressions, natural catastrophes, ecological "sins of omission and commission," and examples of inhumanity, as well as much that gives us hope for the future. We were in the process of continual duelling or jousting with the Soviet Union, a situation in which both sides fully understood the devastation that could be unleashed on mankind. Nevertheless, whether we understood it philosophically, we looked ahead idealistically, realistically, pragmatically, existentially, materialistically, or what have you?

Now conditions have changed. On the home front we seek to control the tides of the economic cycle, also with the understanding that the problem is worldwide. We try to comprehend and then help out with the peaceful and the shooting revolutions and little wars going on all about us. Along with other countries in the United Nations, we now appreciate that there will be an ongoing "war" with terrorism well into the indefinite future. We still hear periodically that automation in the post-industrial world may bring about a service economy where at least one class of people will be paid not to work. However, at the moment this possibility seems rather remote. Nevertheless, education for leisure would seem to warrant serious consideration because it has such import for good in the lives of many people—in the technologically advanced nations at least.

History shows that no civilization has survived for long when the people had too much free time, but perhaps this "principle" is based on too few examples. Some of our citizens (e.g., the ecologists) question penetratingly whether we can continue our unprecedented development as a continent where most people will find happiness and satisfaction despite the fact that we are increasingly crowding people together in megalopolises (i.e., heavily populated cities with sprawling suburbs). To answer these implied questions in relation to the use of leisure, we should examine our philosophical positions (i.e. value orientations) with their possible implications for education, recreation, and other aspects of everyday living. To begin to aid you discover where you fit on this matter of use of leisure, I have briefly summarized several broad positions for consideration on what I have termed a philosophical spectrum. (In the Appendix, you will find a detailed philosophical, self-evaluation test for use either right now or after completing your reading of this book.)

Viewing Leisure Through Differing "Conceptual Lenses"

> Note: *The reader should understand that this is my carefully considered, but unscientific, assessment of the various stances taken by people and groups on the subject of people's involvement in leisure pursuits of varying types.*

Progressivism. Progressivists, who believe that it is only possible to find out if something is worthwhile through experience, initially did not, for example, like the "splintering" that was taking place within the fields of health, physical education, sport, recreation, and dance (i.e., each of the so-called "allied professions" striking out on its own as strongly as possible). So they were initially apt to protest against discussing recreation education for the individual separately from physical education broadly conceived. However, the world is growing increasingly complex, and the separate but overlapping bodies of knowledge undergirding each of the allied professions has made our considerations vary from the macroscopic to the microscopic.

For progressivists, whatever the case may be, education for the worthy use of leisure is basic to the curriculum of the school—a curriculum in which pupil growth, as defined by the philosophical pragmatist, is all-important. Second, play as defined above should foster moral growth, and third, over-organized sport competition is not true or the best kind of recreation, since the welfare of the individual is often relegated to second place. Progressivists make it quite clear that it is a mistake to confuse the psychological distinction between work and play with the traditional economic distinction. (Interestingly, the late J.S. Brubacher placed these concepts on a continuum from frivolity to play to work to drudgery, seemingly most apt distinctions.) All citizens should have ample opportunity to have free time and to use it in a creative and fruitful manner. Progressivists would not condemn a person who watched others perform with a high level of skill in any of our culturally accepted activities, including sport, so long as the individual kept the spectator role in the proper place. Furthermore, they would view with favor a carefully planned program of interscholastic, intercollegiate athletics, or interuniversity athletics that is built on a sound physical education and intramurals sport base within the institution concerned..

Radical Progressivism (earlier known in educational philosophy as Reconstructionism in educational philosophy). This is a (presently utopian) progressivist position that I have arbitrarily placed somewhat to the right of pragmatism because of its doctrine of "defensible partiality." ("Defensible partiality" was defined as the position that a person is obligated to "go along" with majority opinion until such time as he/she can convince others to vote his/her way on an issue or problem.) It embodies the belief that reality is evolving, and that there is no such thing as a pre-established order in the world (identical with philosophic pragmatism, of course). Thus, a fixed or universal curriculum in the programs espoused by the allied professions, including recreation education, is unthinkable.

This curriculum would be developed through the employment of shared planning to determine what specific contributions the allied professions might make to the program of general education and to the preparation for the worthy use of leisure provided. If the community school concept were used, the student could well be offered about an hour and a half in a (total) day for recreation and relaxation alone. "Carry-over" games and sports with opportunities for wholesome educational play would undoubtedly contribute to total fitness. The radical progressivist aim is social-self-realization, which is meant to connote self-realization in a one-world environment. In such a setting, creative artistic expression through recreational activities such as rhythms and dance should be emphasized. Intramural-recreational sports, compared to overly competitive, commercialized inter-institutional athletics, rank high. Democratic method should be used to aid the group to fulfill goals that themselves are the result of democratic consensus. Self-expression is important for human development, and sound recreational use of leisure would promote this particular goal.

Existentialism/Phenomenology. Existentialist thought, has been classified as "progressivistic" primarily because of the fundamental individualism of the approach. It gives play an important place. Personal liberation is highly desirable, of course, and this is most certainly a function of play. In sporting activities individuals can be free as they select their own values, commit themselves to people and causes, and achieve self-expression in the process. Children can create their own world of play and thereby begin to realize their true identities. Obviously, professional sport and university sport that is semiprofessional would be completely antithetical to true existentialists. Existentialists at play want no irrevocably prescribed formations, no coach calling the plays authoritatively and thereby destroying the players' "authenticity," and no fanatical spectators urged on by exploited cheerleaders exhorting them to win at almost any cost.

Traditionalism (Type A & Type B). Traditionalists (Type A) (i.e., perhaps those who are philosophical idealists) have both a firm belief in an intrinsic system of values (including educational values) and an extreme concern with individual personality and its development. They have typically been ambiguous about the role of recreation education in the school and in adult life. Everything considered, it is time for all traditionalists to reassess the contributions that recreation and play can and do make in education, as they define it.

Another difficulty that confronts traditionalists is deciding on the roles of developmental physical activity and recreation education. Perhaps only developmental physical activity should be included in the educational hierarchy, and all other recreational needs and interests should be met by the community recreation program in afterschool programs. On the other hand, a traditionalist might view favorably a theory of recreation and play that grants educational possibilities to these activities.

The self-expression theory of play suggests that the individual's chief need in life is to be able to give expression to her or his own personality—a theory obviously quite compatible with the conception of the person as an organic unity. Idealists believe that the person is a purposive being who is striving to achieve those values in life that are embedded in reality. To the extent that idealists can realize the eternal values through the choice of the right kinds of play and recreation without flouting the moral order in the world, they may become progressive enough to downplay the traditional dualistic theory of work and play—a theory that has both plagued and challenged North American education down to the present day.

There are distinct signs that specific Protestant denominations are becoming increasingly aware of the role that sound, purposeful recreation can play in the promulgation of the Christian idealistic way of life. In North America such recognition has been largely a 20th-century phenomenon. The field of recreation has developed to the point where it is now clearly one of the major social institutions in North American life. If "the ideal suggests the integrated individual in an integrated society growing in the image of the integrated universe," (as defined by Horne earlier) then all types of sound recreational experience and activity can seemingly make a contribution to the realization of this ideal. We are warned that we North Americans are faced with a "recreational imperative."

Traditionalists (Type B)—i.e., those who are perhaps philosophical realists—accept the world at face value. They believe that our experiencing it changes it not one whit. They sharply differentiate between work and play. Play serves a useful purpose at recess or after school, but it should not be part of the regular curriculum. They would agree that the use of leisure is significant to the development of our culture, but they would also be quick to point out that the United States will only maintain its leading position by a lot more hard work and somewhat less leisure on the part of the large majority. They see leisure pursuits or experience as an opportunity to get relief from work—opportunities that serve a re-creative purpose in life.

The well-known surplus energy theory of play and recreation makes sense to these "Type B" people. So does the bio-social theory of play—the idea that play helps the organism achieve balance. They would tend to deprecate the fact that the play attitude seems to be missing almost completely in many organized sports. Play (and recreation) are therefore very important to philosophic "realists"; it should be "liberating," with people developing their potentialities for wholesome hobbies through recreation. As they see it, recreation can serve as a safety valve for the reduction of life's psychic tensions. Even though play should not be considered as an integral or basic part of the curriculum, we should not forget that it provides an indispensable seasoning to the good life by helping to improve the quality of living. Extracurricular play and recreational activities and a sound general education should suffice to equip the student for leisure activities in our society.

Analytic Philosophy. By the middle of the 20th century, an approach dubbed as "philosophy in a new key" was in full bloom. It involved those who employed an "analytic" methodology with their "doing" of philosophy, an approach that has been called analytic philosophy, conceptual analysis, language analysis, philosophical analysis, etc. These scholars were— many are still—in the British tradition that began around the turn of the twentieth century with such philosophers as Bertrand Russell and G.E. Moore. They turned their backs on the more traditional "categorizations" of twentieth- century philosophy mentioned above. because they believed that such an approach was too inexact. They simply did not delineate carefully and clearly the essential elements necessary for clarification of problems and issues.

While the approach used by me (and many others) above may indeed be less "scientific" and more metaphysical in its method of defining values, ethics, and morality (except for pragmatism), it is difficult to fully understand why the "new-key, analytic group" in my field of physical education/kinesiology have persisted for more than a generation now to emulate many of their colleagues from other disciplines (i.e., main-stream philosophy and educational philosophy). I say this because, in so doing, they have almost completely removed themselves from "the battlefield of ideas" in the profession. As a result, along with mainstream philosophy, they have collaborated in the sharp departure from consideration of life's everyday important problems. Thus, untold millions of people around the world are leading their lives based on a combination of some "handed-down" religious or ideological stance coupled with common sense. The shallowness of commonsense is certainly well known by most educated people, of course, and the imprecise, ethereal quality of religions' pronouncements about life and living often leave much to be desired in the realm of play and recreational activities.

This is not to say that analytic philosophy in its several versions has not made a definite contribution to humankind. A solid example of what was called conceptual language analysis, for example, was initially provided by the philosopher James Keating (1964, p. 28). He was the first to explain to the physical education profession that etymologically the terms "sport" and "athletics" had completely different derivations. Of course, this is a valid distinction that should be made. The athletes are the prize hunters, and the sportsmen and sportswomen become involved to maximize the sportive occasion for both parties or teams involved. However, it is obvious that people confuse this issue daily by misuse of these terms. Although righting this mistake in language is now an impossibility in everyday parlance, it would help greatly if our sporting games and contests could be categorized as to make it clear what the true objective of the contest should be. (I am not holding my breath waiting for this to happen.)

14. FORECASTING THE FUTURE

Everything that we have discussed above either of an optimistic or pessimistic nature leads us to one conclusion. We had best be ready for the ever-present change that is occurring. "Getting in league with the future' can initially be carried out best, I presume, by making a sincere, solid effort to understand what futuristics or futurology is all about. From there one could take the next step and apply these findings to one aspect of our lives—in this case, the possible future of the allied professions of health, physical education, recreation, sport, and dance. Here, then, I turn first for some guidance to *Visions of the future,* a publication of the well-known Hudson Institute (1984). Initially, we are urged to tailor our thinking to three ways of looking at the future: (1) the possible future, (2) the probable future, and (3) the preferable future (p. 4).

The "Possible," "Probable," and "Preferable" Futures

As you might imagine, the possible future includes everything that could happen, and thus perceptions of the future must be formed by us individually and collectively. The probable future refers to occurrences that are likely to happen, and so here the range of alternatives must be considered. Finally, the preferable future relates to an approach whereby people make choices, thereby indicating how they would like things to happen. Underlying all of this are certain basic assumptions or premises such as (1) that the future hasn't been predetermined by some force or power; (2) that the future cannot be accurately predicted because we don't understand the process of change that fully; and (3) that the future will undoubtedly be influenced by choices that people make, but won't necessarily turn out the way they want it to be (Amara, 1981).

As we all appreciate, people have been predicting the future for thousands of years, undoubtedly with a limited degree of success. Considerable headway has been made, of course, since the time when animal entrails were examined to provide insight about the future (one of the techniques of so-called divination). Nowadays, for example, methods of prediction include forecasting by the use of trends and statistics. One most recent approaches along these these lines has been of great interest to me because I have been using a variation of this technique for more than 50 years with a persistent problems approach (originated by John S. Brubacher, 1947) leading to ongoing analyses of my own field (Zeigler, 1964, 1968, 1977, 1979, 1989). Here I am referring to the work of John Naisbitt and The Naisbitt Group as described above (and originally in *Megatrends*, 1982). These people believe that "the most reliable way to anticipate the future is by understanding the present" (p. 2). Hence they monitor occurrences all over the world through a technique of descriptive method known as content analysis. They actually monitor the amount of space given to various topics in newspapers—an approach they feel is valid because "the news-reporting process is forced choice in a closed system" (p. 4).

Melnick and associates, in *Visions of the future* (1984), discuss a further aspect of futuristics—the question of "levels of certainty." They explain that the late Herman Kahn, an expert in this area, often used the term "Scotch Verdict" when he was concerned about the level of certainty available prior to making a decision. This idea was borrowed from the Scottish system of justice in which a person charged with the commission of a crime can be found "guilty," "not guilty," or "not been proven guilty." This "not been proven guilty" (or "Scotch") verdict implies there is enough evidence to demonstrate that the person charged is guilty, but that insufficient evidence has been presented to end all reasonable doubt about the matter. Hence a continuum has been developed at one end of which we can state we are absolutely sure (100%) that such-and-such is not true. Accordingly, at the other end of the continuum we can state we are absolutely sure (100%) that such-and-such is the case (pp. 6-7). Obviously, inbetween these two extremes are gradations of the level of certainty. From here this idea has been carried over to the realm of future forecasting.

Stages of the "Great Transition" Taking Place

Next we are exhorted to consider the "Great Transition" that humankind has been experiencing, how there has been a pre-industrial stage, an industrial stage and, finally, a post-industrial stage that appears to be arriving in North America first. Each of the stages has its characteristics that must be recognized. For example, in pre-industrial society there was slow population growth, people lived simply with very little money, and the forces of nature made life very difficult. When the industrial stage or so-called modernization entered the picture, population growth was rapid, wealth increased enormously, and people became increasingly less vulnerable to the destructive forces of nature. The assumption here, of course, is that comprehension of the transition that is occurring can give us some insight as to what the future might hold—not that we can be "100% sure," but at least we might be able to achieve a "Scotch Verdict" (p. 47). If North America is that part of the world that is the most economically and technologically advanced, and as a result will complete the Great Transition by becoming a post-industrial culture, then we must be aware of what this will mean to our society. Melnick explains that we have probably already entered a "super-industrial period" of the Industrial Stage in which "projects will be very large scale; services will be readily available, efficient and sophisticated; people will have vastly increased leisure time; and many new technologies will be created" (pp. 35-37).

It is important that we understand what is happening as we move further forward into what presumably is the final or third stage of the Great Transition. First, it should be made clear that the level of certainty here in regard to predictions is at Kahn's "Scotch Verdict" point on the continuum. The world has never faced this situation before; so we don't know exactly how to date the beginning of such a stage. Nevertheless, it seems to be taking place right now (the super-industrial period having started after World War II). As predicted, those developments mentioned above (e.g., services readily available) appear to be continuing. It is postulated that population growth is slower than it was 20 years ago; yet, it is true that people are living longer. Next it is estimated that a greater interdependence among nations and the steady development of new technologies will contribute to a steadily improving economic climate for underdeveloped nations. Finally, it is forecast that advances in science and accompanying technology will bring almost innumerable technologies to the fore that will affect life styles immeasurably all over the world.

This discussion could continue almost indefinitely, but the important points to be made here are emerging rapidly. First, we need a different way of looking at the subject of so-called natural resources. In this interdependent world, this "global village" if you will, natural resources are more than just the sum of raw materials. They include also the beneficial application of technology, the organizational bureaucracy to cope with the materials, and the resultant usefulness of the resource that creates supply and demand (p. 74). The point seems to be that the total resource picture (as explained here) is reasonably optimistic if correct decisions are made about raw materials, energy, food production, and use of the environment. These are admittedly rather large "IFS" (pp. 73-97).

Two Types of Problems to Overcome

Finally, the need to understand global problems of two types is stressed. One group is called "mostly understandable problems," and they are solvable. Here reference is made to:

1) population growth,

2) natural resource issues,

3) acceptable environmental health,

4) shift in society's economic base to service occupations, and

5) effect of advanced technology.

It is the second group classified as "mostly uncertain problems" that creates the most concern. These are the problems that could bring on disaster. First, the Great Transition is affecting the entire world, and the eventual outcome of this new type of cultural change is uncertain. Thus, we must be ready for these developments attitudinally. Second, in this period of changing values and attitudes, people in the various countries and cultures have much to learn and they will have to make great adjustments as well. Third, there is the danger that society will—possibly unwittingly—stumble into some irreversible environmental catastrophe (e.g., upper-atmosphere ozone depletion). Fourth, the whole problem of weapons, wars, and terrorism, and whether the world will be able to stave off all-out nuclear warfare. Fifth, and finally, whether bad luck and bad management will somehow block the entire world from undergoing the Great Transition successfully—obviously a great argument for the development of management art and science (pp. 124-129).

15. A FINAL WORD

What can be said—what should be said—to bring this discussion to a proper conclusion, at least a tentative one for the present? I knew in 1967 that the world was changing when I wrote about the coming age of leisure. As it turned out, I just didn't know how much it would change by the end of the century—and how rapidly such major change would occur! A revised definition of "the good life" appears to be in order as we enter the 21st century. Life today is characterized by so much more uncertainty for youth than previously (Zeigler, 1997).

This means that the goal today is still to help people of all ages to learn that the many educational and recreational program objectives can help them "live the good life," the best possible one available. However, in the final analysis, people will need to search individually for this elusive goal. Personally I have developed a tentative list of what I believe a person should strive for over the years in the search for "the mythical good life." My list consists of the following eight "directives" for you, the reader to consider in your own quest:

1. Work to develop desirable personality and character traits based on sound personal and professional ethics,

2. Seek to attain a broad general education in the humanities, social sciences, and natural sciences,

3. Follow up with intensive, specialized professional preparation in a field that really interests you,

4. Strive to maintain successful human relations with family, friends, and professional colleagues,

5. Practice good health habits and maintain at least an "irreducible-minimum" level of physical fitness through planned exercise, sport, and physical recreation involvement,

6. As you can, and do try to plan for it, give volunteer service to your community and your profession,

7. Enjoy active and creative recreational participation (i.e., physical, social, aesthetic & creative, communicative, and "learning" recreational interests), and

8. Develop a life purpose based on dedicated, ethical professional practice.

Additionally, I developed two types of tests for you, the reader, to try out. The first evaluative device you completed early on in this book. It was the recreational self-evaluation questionnaire by which you were able to assess what contribution wholesome recreation is, or is not, making to your life at this time . The results, or score, that you obtained was objective in one sense (e.g., 35 pts.). However, in the final analysis what you discovered should be viewed subjectively. You would probably need a 32-hour day (or more!) to be a consistent scorer of 50 pts. In fact, you might not even want to strive for—say—40 or 45 points. And, if so, who is to say that you are or are not leading an interesting, fulfilling life? In the final analysis, this must be a personal decision.

The philosophic self-evaluation test (Appendix, p. 74 et ff.) will help you discover the possible consistency (or inconsistency) of your basic value orientation. This is a philosophical, self-evaluation checklist that may be used either by a person seriously interested in the place of recreation in his or her leisure pattern. It is titled "What Do I Believe?" I urge you to undergo this quite stringent self-evaluation of your beliefs. I urge you to carry through with this self-evaluation questionnaire right now. From time to time, especially as a person enters a new stage of life, he or she should re-evaluate personal values and goals in keeping with his or her beliefs about the prevailing—but ever changing—social system. Such re-evaluation should be correlated with the changes that are occurring with the individual's own traits, characteristics, and abilities at a particular stage of life.

Finally, in addition to these personal assessments, including the above suggestions for "becoming happy and successful" in your personal and professional life, we as enlightened individuals or professionals will also need to strive collectively, working together as partners, to maintain North America (Canada and the United States) as a truly fine place to live as we work and strive for "the good life."

Despite the obvious good sense of people striving diligently for distinct and/or greater status in our obviously increasing state of multi-ethnicity in both the United States and Canada, we will only continue to be one of the world's best places to live to the extent that we proudly state that we—in our respective countries—are Americans or Canadians first and whatever else second. There can be no other way at this time as we search for the unity and "the good life" that we hope that all people on earth may also be privileged to find some day.

NOTES

1. Schor's contention of the "overworked American" was supported in a "Viewpoint" statement to *The New York Times* on Aug. 29, 1993. However, this position was immediately challenged by Charles D.   Wertheim in a letter to the editor ("What Overworked American?") of *The New York Times*, Sept. 12, 1993, in which Wertheim states the following:

"Consider the following figures, drawn not from fantasy but from American industry. If, from the 52-week year, you deduct four weeks' vacation, two weeks of personal or sick days, and 10 holidays, that leaves only 44 weeks worked. At 35 hours per week, this totals 1,540 gross hours—no deductions for coffee breaks, etc., which usually are significant. The total brings the United States down to the second lowest in manufacturing hours in the industrial world from second highest.

Your article's 1923 hourly total represents probably the most extreme in one direction. My figures are probably extreme in the other. But even an average number would disprove your assumptions."

It seems obvious that more careful investigation of this issue is warranted.

2. One of the best statements of the (naive) naturalistic position was made by Spencer (1949; originally 1861) in one of his four famous essays on education, "What knowledge is of most worth?" Written at a time when he was arguing for inclusion of science as the most important aspect of the educational curriculum, Spencer used the phrase "complete living" as the general aim of education. In listing activities in "their true order of subordination," he recognized that the individual has a responsibility to use leisure wisely so as to enjoy what he called "complete living" (pp. 305-307).

REFERENCES

Aburdene, P. & Naisbitt, J. (1992). *Megatrends for women*. NY: Villard Books.

Allentuck, A.(1995) Get ready for more leisure time, *The Globe and Mail* (Toronto), p. C19.

Amara, R. (1981). The futures field., February.

Berelson, B. & Steiner G.A. (1964). *Human behavior: An inventory of scientific findings*. NY: Harcourt, Brace & World.

Brubacher, J.S. (1966). *A history of the problems of education* (2nd ed.). New York: McGraw-Hill. *Business Work* (Special Report). (Oct. 17, 1994). Rethinking work, pp. 17-117.

Campau, D. (1967). Is Canada cultured? *Saturday Review*, Feb. 11, 20-22.

Cousins, N. (1974). Prophecy and pessimism. *Saturday Review-World*, Aug. 24, 1974, 6-7.

Commager, H.S. (1966). *Freedom and order*. NY: G. Braziller.

Csikszentmihalyi, M. (1993). *The evolving self.* NY: HarperCollins.

Durant, W. & A. (1968). *The lessons of history*. NY: Simon & Schuster.

Godbey G. (1992). Leisure policy in the 1990s. In *The Changing Patterns of Work and Leisure*. Burlington, Ontario: Society of Directors of Municipal Recreation of Ontario.

Huntington, H.P. (June 6, 1993). World politics entering a new phase, *The New York Times*, E19.

Holiday (Editorial). (1956), March, 1956.

Huxley, J. (Jan., 1967). The crisis in man's destiny. *Playboy*, 93-94, 212-217.

Kateb, G. (1965). Utopia and the good life. *Daedalus*, 24, 2:454-473.

Kekes, J. (Jan. 1987). Is our morality disintegrating? *Public Affairs Quarterly*, 1, 1:79-94.

Lawlor, J. (Sept. 3, 1993). "Workers want to get a life, *USA Today*, Sec. B, 1-2.

Lenk, H. (1994). Value changes in the achieving society: A social-philosophical perspective. In *Organisation for Economic Co-operation and Development* (Ed.), OECD societies in transition (pp. 81-94).

Lipset, S.M. (1973). National character. In D. Koulack & D. Perlman (Eds.), *Readings in social psychology::Focus on Canada* (Chap. 1). Toronto: Wiley.

Marx, L. (1990). Does improved technology mean progress? In A.H. Teich, (Ed.), *Technology and the future* (5th Ed.) (pp. 3-14). (1990). NY: St. Martin's.

Melnick, R. (1984). *Visions of the future*. Croton-on-Hudson, NY: Hudson Institute.

Mesthene, E.G. (1990). The role of technology in society. In A.H. Teich, (Ed.). *Technology and the future* (5th Ed.) (pp. 77-99). (1990). NY: St. Martin's.

Michael, D.N. (1962). *Cybernation: the silent conquest*. Santa Barbara, CA: Center for the Study of Democratic Institutions.

Morris, V.C. (1956). Physical education and the philosophy of education. *Journal of Health, Physical Education and Recreation*, 27, 3:21-22, 30-31.

Naisbitt, J. (1982). *Megatrends*. New York: Warner.

Nakamoto, M. (Nov. 13, 1993). Workaholic Japanese told to get a life, *The Financial Post* (Canada), p. 15.

Nash, J.B. (1953). *Philosophy of recreation and leisure*. St. Louis: The C.V. Mosby Co.

Reid D. & Mannell, R. (1990). Changing patterns of work, non-work and leisure. In *The Changing Patterns of Work and Leisure*. Burlington, Ontario: Society of Directors of Municipal Recreation of Ontario.

Rifkin, J. (1995). *The end of work*. NY: Putnam & Sons.

Rousseau, J.J. (1943). *Emile*. London: J.M. Dent.

Royal Bank of Canada Monthly Letter, The. (1961). In search of a happy life. 42, 3:1-4.

Schlesinger, A.M., Jr. (1998, Rev. & Enl. Ed.). *The disuniting of America: Reflections on a multicultural society.*. NY; W.W. Norton.

Schor, J. (1992). *The overworked American: The unexpected decline of leisure*. NY: Basic Books.

Simpson, G.G. (1949). *The meaning of evolution*. New Haven & London: Yale University Press.

Spencer, H. (1949; orig. publ. in 1861). *Education: Intellectual, moral, and physical*. London: C.A. Watts.

Teich, A.H. (1990). *Technology and the future*. NY: St. Martin's Press.

Ten events that shook the world between 1984 and 1994. (Special Report). *Utne Reader,* 62 (March/April 1994):58-74.

Time Essay. (1967). Canada discovers itself, May 5.

Time Essay. (1992). Canada 2000: Reflections on what's ahead, December 14.

Utne Reader. (July-Aug. 1993). "For love or money," 46:66-87.

Walz, J. (1967). Ambitious tasks set by Pearson. *The New York Times,* May 7.

Zeigler, E.F. (1967). L'enigme du monde de demain: Comment mener une bonne vie. Mouvement, 2: 5-14. (This paper was also published in *CAHPER Journal* (Canada), 34, 2:3-8, Jan. 1968.)

Zeigler, E.F. (1975). *Personalizing physical education and sport philosophy*. Champaign, IL: Stipes.

Zeigler, E.F. (1986). *Assessing sport and physical education: Diagnosis and projection*. Champaign, IL: Stipes.

Zeigler, E.F. (1988). *History of physical education and sport* (Rev. ed.). Champaign, IL: Stipes. (Selected chapters were written by M.L. Howell, R. Howell, R. G. Glassford, G. Redmond, R.K. Barney, and G.A. Paton.)

Zeigler, E.F. (1989). *Sport and physical education philosophy. Carmel,* IN: Benchmark Press.

Zeigler, E.F. (1990). *Sport and physical education: Past, present, future*. Champaign, IL: Stipes.

Zeigler. E.F. (2002). *Who knows what's right anymore: A guide to personal decision-making*. Victoria, Canada: Trafford

Zeldin, T. (1994). *An intimate history of humanity*. NY: HarperCollins.

APPENDIX

WHAT DO I BELIEVE?
(A self-evaluation checklist)

Note: I need to alert you to the fact that this "self-evaluation" is a highly subjective matter. I first developed this "personal examination" approximately 50 years ago and have updated it periodically since to the best of my ability.

Instructions: Read the statements below carefully, section by section, and indicate by an (X) the statement in each section that seems closest to your personal belief.

Check your answers only after all SIX sections have been completed. Then complete the summarizing tally on the answer page. Take note of apparent inconsistencies in your overall position.

Finally, check with the freedom-constraint spectrum at the end to discover your educational and philosophic "location," whether in the center, the right or the left.

Note: Many of the words, terms, phrases, etc. have been obtained from the work of philosophers, educational philosophers, recreation philosophers, and sport and physical education philosophers, living or deceased. I am most grateful for this assistance, but finally decided not to mention their names individually throughout this test so as not to possibly prejudice the person taking the test. Their names are listed individually at the end, but as a group of names. In this self-evaluation check list, the professional sections were delimited to the professions of recreation and physical education & educational sport.

Keep in mind that I am not seeking to make the case that, for example, a position taken under Category 1 will result by logical deduction in a comparable position being taken in a following category either within the education, recreation education, or physical education & educational sport categories. Nevertheless, positions taken in these latter categories should, to be consistent, probably be grounded on philosophical presuppositions stated earlier.

Category I

THE NATURE OF REALITY (METAPHYSICS)

A. _____ Experience and nature constitute both the form and the content of the entire universe. There is no such thing as a pre-established order of affairs in the world. Reality is evolving, and humanity appears to be a most important manifestation of the natural process. The impact of cultural forces upon people is fundamental, and every effort should be made to understand them as we strive to build the best type of a group-centered culture. In other words, the structure of cultural reality should be our foremost concern. Cultural determinants have shaped human history, and a crucial stage has now been reached in the development of life on the planet. Our efforts must now be focused on the building of a world culture.

B. _____ I believe that the metaphysical and normative types of philosophizing have lost their basis for justification in the 21st century. Their presumed wisdom has not been able to withstand the rigor of careful analysis. Sound theory is available to humankind through the application of scientific method to problem-solving. Thus, what is the exact nature of philosophy? Who is in a position to answer the ultimate questions about the nature of reality? The scientist is, of course, and the philosopher must become the servant of science through conceptual analysis and the rational reconstruction of language. Accordingly, the philosopher must resign himself or herself to dealing with important, but lesser, questions than the origin of the universe and the nature of the human being— and what implications this might have for everyday conduct.

C. _____ The world of men and women is a human one, and it is from the contest of this human world that all the abstractions of science ultimately derive their meaning. There is the world of material objects, of course, that extends in mathematical space with only quantitative and measurable properties, but we humans are first and foremost "concrete involvements" within the world. Existence precedes essence, and it is up to men and women to decide their fate. This presumably makes the human different from all other creatures on Earth. It appears true that people can actually transform life's present condition, and thus the future may well stand open to these unusual beings.

D. _____ Nature is an emergent evolution, and the human's frame of reality is limited to nature as it functions. The world is characterized by activity and change. Rational man and woman have developed through organic evolution over millions of years, and the world is yet incomplete. It is a reality that is constantly undergoing change because of a theory of emergent novelty that appears to be operating within the universe. People do enjoy true freedom of will. This freedom is achieved through continuous and developmental learning from experience.

E. _____ Mind as experienced by all people is basic and real. The entire universe is mind, essentially. The human is more than just a body; people possess souls, and such possession makes them of a higher order than all other creatures on Earth. The order of the world is due to the manifestation in space and time of an eternal and spiritual reality. The individual is simply part of the whole. It is therefore a person's duty to learn as much about the Absolute as possible. Within this position there is divided opinion regarding the problem of monism or pluralism (one force or more than one force at work). The individual person has freedom to determine which way he or she will go in life. The individual can relate to the moral law in the universe, or he or she can turn against it.

F. _____ The world exists in itself, apart from our desires and knowledge. There is only one reality—that which we perceive is it. The universe is made up of real substantial entities, existing in themselves and ordered to one another by extramental relations. Some feel there is one basic unity present, while others holding this position believe in a non-unified cosmos with two or more substances or processes at work. Things don't just happen; they happen because many interrelated forces make them occur in a particular way. People live within this world of cause and effect. They simply cannot make things happen independent of it.

Category II

ETHICS AND MORALITY (Axiology/Values)

A. _____ The source of all human experience lies in the regularities of the universe. Things don't just happen; they happen because many interrelated forces make them occur in a particular way. Humans in this environment are confronted by one reality only—that which we perceive is it! The "life of reason" is extremely important, a position that emanates originally from Aristotle who placed intellectual virtues above moral virtues in his hierarchy. Many holding this stance believe that all elements of nature, including people, are inextricably linked in an endless chain of causes and effects. Thus, they accept a sort of ethical determinism—i.e., what people are morally is determined by response patterns imprinted in their being by both heredity and environment. A large number in the world carry this fundamental position still further by adding a theological component; for them the highest good is ultimate union with God, the Creator, who is responsible for teleological and supernatural reality. Human goodness is reached by the spirituality of the form attained as the individual achieves emancipation from the material (or the corporeal). The belief is that a person's being contains potential energy that may be guided or directed toward God or away from Him; thus, what the individual does in the final analysis determines whether such action will be regarded as right or wrong.

B. _____ There should be no distinction between moral goods and natural goods. There has long been a facts/values dualism in existence, and this should be eradicated as soon as possible by the use of scientific method applied to ethical situations. Thus, we should employ reflective thinking to obtain the ideas that will function as tentative solutions for the solving of life's concrete problems. Those ideas can serve as hypotheses to be tested in life. If the ideas work in solving problematic situations, they become true. In this way we have empirical verification of hypotheses tending to bring theory and practice into a closer union. When we achieve agreement in factual belief, agreement in attitudes should soon follow. In this way science can ultimately bring about complete agreement on factual belief or knowledge about human behavior. Thus there will be a continuous adaptation of values to the culture's changing needs that will in turn bring about the directed reconstruction of all social institutions.

C. _____ The problems of ethics should be resolved quite differently than they have throughout most of history. Ethics cannot be resolved completely through the application of scientific method, although an ethical dispute must be on a factual level—i.e., factual statements must be distinguished from value statements. Ethics should be normative in the sense that we have moral standards. However, this is a difficult task because the term "good" appears to be indefinable. The terms used to define or explain ethical standards or norms should be analyzed logically in a careful manner. Social scientists should be enlisted to help in the determination of the validity of factual statements, as well as in the analysis of conflicting attitudes as progress is determined. Ethical dilemmas in modern life can be resolved through the combined efforts of the philosophical moralist and the scientist. The resultant beliefs may in time change people's attitudes. Basically, the task is to establish a hierarchy of reasons with a moral basis.

D. _____ Good and bad and rightness and wrongness, are relative and vary according to the situation or culture involved (i.e., the needs of a situation are there and then in that society or culture). Each ethical decision is highly individual, initially at least, since every situation has its particularity. The free, authentic individual decides to accept responsibility when he or she responds to a human situation and seeks to answer the need of an animal, person, or group. How does the "witness react to the world?" Guidance in the making of an ethical decision may come either from "outside," from intuition, from one's conscience, from reason, from empirical investigation, etc. Thus it can be argued that there are no absolutely valid ethical principles or universal laws.

E. _____ Ethics and morality are based on cosmic laws, and we are good if we figure out how to share actively in them. If we have problems of moral conduct, we have merely to turn to the Lord's commandments for solutions to all moral problems. Yet there is nothing deterministic here, because the individual himself or herself has an active role to play in determining which ethical actions will bring him or her into closer unity with the supreme Self. However, God is both the source and the goal of the values for which we strive in our everyday lives. In this approach the presence of evil in the world is recognized as a real human experience to be met and conquered. The additional emphasis here is on logical argument to counter the ever-present threat of the philosophy of science. This is countered by the argument that there is unassailable moral law inherent in the universe that presents people with obligations to duty (e.g., honesty is a good that is universal).

F. ____ Our social environment is inextricably related to the many struggles of peoples for improvement of the quality of life—how to place more good in our lives than bad, so to speak. We are opposed to any theory that delineates values as absolute and separates them from everyday striving within a social milieu. Actually, the truth of values can be determined by established principles of evidence. In an effort to achieve worldwide consensus on any and all values, our stated positions on issues and controversial matters must necessarily be criticized in public forums. Cultural realities that affect values should be reoriented through the achievement of agreed-upon purposes (i.e., through social consensus and social-self-realization on a worldwide basis). The goal, then, is to move toward a comprehensive pattern of values that provides both flexibility and variety. This should be accompanied by sufficient freedom to allow the individual to achieve individual and social values in his or her life. However, we must not forget that the majority does rule in evolving democracies, and at times wrong decisions are made. Keeping in mind that the concept of democracy will prevail only to the extent that "enlightened" decisions are made, we must guarantee the ever-present role of the critical minority as it seeks to alter any consensus established. A myth or utopian vision should guide our efforts as we strive toward the achievement of truly human ethical values in the life experiences of all our citizens.

Category III

EDUCATIONAL AIMS AND OBJECTIVES

A. ____ Socialization of the child has become equally as important as his or her intellectual development as a key educational aim in this century. There should be concern, however, because many educational philosophers seem to assume the position that children are to be fashioned so that they will conform to a prior notion of what they should be. Even the progressivists seem to have failed in their effort to help the learner "posture himself or herself." If it does become possible to get general agreement on a set of fundamental dispositions to be formed, should the criterion employed for such evaluation be a public one, rather than personal and private? Education should seek to "awaken awareness" in the learner—awareness of the person as a single subjectivity in the world. Increased emphasis is needed on the arts and social sciences, and the student should freely and creatively choose his or her own pattern of education.

B._____ Social-self-realization is the supreme value in education. The realization of this ideal is most important for the individual in the social setting—a world culture. Positive ideals should be molded toward the evolving democratic ideal by a general education that is group-centered and in which the majority determines the acceptable goals. However, once that majority opinion is determined, all are obligated to conform until such majority opinion can be reversed (the doctrine of "defensible partiality"). Nevertheless, education by means of "hidden coercion" is to be scrupulously avoided. Learning itself is explained by the organismic principle of functional psychology. Acquired social intelligence teaches people to control and direct their urges as they concur with or attempt to modify cultural purposes.

C. ____ The concept of education has become much more complex than was ever realized. Because of the various meanings of the term "education," talking about educational aims and objectives is almost a hopeless task unless a myriad of qualifications is used for clarification. The term "education" has now become what is called a "family-resemblance" one in philosophy. Thus we need to qualify our meaning to explain to the listener whether we mean (1) the subjectmatter; (2) the activity of education carried on by teachers; (3) the process of being educated (or learning) that is occurring; (4) the result, actual or intended, or #2 and #3 taking place through the employment of that which comprises #1 above; (5) the discipline, or field of inquiry and investigation; and (6) the profession whose members are involved professionally with all of the aspects of education described above. With this understanding, it is then possible to make some determination about which specific objectives the profession of education should strive for as it moves in the direction of the achievement of long-range aims.

D. ____ The general aim of education is more education. Education in the broadest sense can be nothing else than the changes made in human beings by their experience. Participation by students in the formation of aims and objectives is absolutely essential to generate the all-important desired interest required for the finest educational process to occur. Social efficiency (i.e., societal socialization) can well be considered the general aim of education. Pupil growth is a paramount goal. This means that the individual is placed at the center of the educational experience.2

E. _____ A philosophy holding that the aim of education is the acquisition of verified knowledge of the environment. Such education involves recognition of the value of content as well as of the activities involved and takes into account the external determinants of human behavior. Education is the acquisition of the art of the utilization of knowledge. The primary task of education is to transmit knowledge, knowledge without which civilization could not continue to flourish. Whatever people have discovered to be true because it conforms to reality should be handed down to future generations as the social or cultural tradition. (Some holding this philosophy believe that the good life emanates from cooperation with God's grace, and further believe that the development of the Christian virtues is obviously of greater worth than learning or anything else.)

F. _____ Through education, the developing organism becomes what it latently is. All education may be said to have a religious significance, the meaning of which is that there is a "moral imperative" on education. As the person's mind strives to realize itself, there is the possibility of the Absolute within the individual mind. Education should aid the child to adjust to the basic realities (the spiritual ideals of truth, beauty, and goodness) that the history of the race has furnished us. The basic values of human living are health, character, social justice, skill, art, love, knowledge, philosophy, and religion.

Category IV

THE EDUCATIVE PROCESS (Epistemology)

A. _____ Understanding the nature of knowledge will clarify the nature of reality. Nature is the medium by which the Absolute communicates to us. Basically, knowledge comes only from the mind, a mind which must offer and receive ideas. Mind and matter are qualitatively different. A finite mind emanates through heredity from another finite mind. Thought is the standard by which all else in the world is judged. An individual attains truth for himself or herself by examining the wisdom of the past through his or her mind. Reality, viewed in this way, is a system of logic and order that has been established by the Universal Mind. Experimental testing helps to determine what the truth really is.

B. _____ The child experiences an "awareness of being" in his/her subjective life about the time of puberty—and is never the same thereafter. The young person truly becomes aware of his or her existence, and the fact that there is now a responsibility for one's own conduct. After this point in life, education must be an "act of discovery" to be truly effective. Somehow the teacher should help the young person to become involved personally with his or her education, and also with the world situation in which such an education is taking place. Objective or subjective knowledge should be personally selected and appropriated by the youth unto himself or herself, or else it will be relatively meaningless in that particular life. Thus it matters not whether logic, scientific evidence, sense perception, intuition, or revelation is claimed as the basis of knowledge acquisition, no learning will take place for that individual self until the child or young person decides that such learning is "true" for him or her. Therefore the young person knows when he or she knows!

C. _____ Knowledge is the result of a process of thought with a useful purpose. Truth is not only to be tested by its correspondence with reality, but also by its practical results. Knowledge is earned through experience and is an instrument of verification. Mind has evolved in the natural order as a more flexible means whereby people adapt themselves to the world, Learning takes place when interest and effort unite to produce the desired result. A psychological order of learning (problem-solving as explained through scientific method) is ultimately more useful than a logical arrangement (proceeding from the simple fact to the complex conclusion). However, we shouldn't forget that there is always a social context to learning, and the curriculum itself should be adapted to the particular society for which it is intended.

D. _____ Concern with the educative process should begin with an understanding of the terms that are typically employed for discussion purposes within any educational program. The basic assumption is that these terms are usually employed loosely and often improperly. For example, to be precise we should be explaining that a student is offered educational experiences in a classroom and/or laboratory setting. Through the employment of various types and techniques of instructional methodology (e.g., lectures), he or she hears facts, increases the scope of information and/or knowledge, and learns to comprehend and interpret the material (understanding). Possessing various kinds and amounts of ability or aptitude, students gradually develop competencies and a certain degree or level of skill. It is hoped that certain appreciations about the worth of the individual student's experiences will be developed, and that he or she will form certain attitudes about familial, societal, and professional life that lie ahead. Finally, societal values and norms, with other social influences, will help educators, fulfilling role within their collectivities and subcollectivities, determine the best methods (with accompanying experimentation, of course) of achieving socially acceptable educational goals.

E. _____ An organismic approach to the learning process is basic. Thought cannot be independent of certain aspects of the organism. This is because thought is related integrally with emotional and muscular functions. The person's mind enables him or her to cope with the problems of human life in a social environment within a physical world. Social intelligence is actually closely related to scientific method. Certain operational concepts, inseparable from metaphysics and axiology (beliefs about reality and values), focus on the reflective thought, problem-solving, and social consensus necessary for the gradual transformation of the culture.

F. _____ There are two major learning (epistemological) theories of knowledge in this philosophical stance. One states that the aim of knowledge is to bring into awareness the object as it really is. The other emphasizes that objects are "represented" in the human's consciousness, not "presented." Students should develop habits and skills involved with acquiring knowledge, with using knowledge practically to meet life's problems, and with realizing the enjoyment that life offers. A second variation of learning theory (epistemological belief) here indicates that the child develops his or her intellect by employing reason to learn a subject. The principal educational aims proceeding hand in hand with learning theory here would be the same for all people at all times in all places. Others with a more religious orientation holding this position, basically add to this stance that education is the process by which people seek to link themselves ultimate with their Creator.

Category V

VALUES IN RECREATION (EDUCATION)

A. _____ As I see it, work and play are typically sharply differentiated in life. Play serves a most useful purpose at recess or after school, but it should not be part of the regular curriculum. I believe that the use of leisure is significant to the development of our culture, but I realize today that improved educational achievement is going to take a lot more hard work and somewhat less leisure. I see leisure pursuits as an opportunity to get relief from work while serving a re-creative purpose in human life. So does the more recent bio-scoial theory of play—the idea that play helps the organism to achieve balance. I feel that the "play attitude" is missing almost completely in most competitive sports. Play (and recreation) are, therefore, very important to me; I believe they should be "liberating" to the individual. People can develop their potentialities for wholesome hobbies through recreation. Further, recreation can serve as a "safety valve" by the reduction of the psychic tensions that are evidently caused by so many of life's typical stresses. In sum, even though play should not be considered as a basic part of the curriculum, we should not forget that it provides an "indispensable seasoning" to the good life. Along with a sound general education, extra-curricular play and recreational activities should suffice to equip the student for leisure activities in our society.

B. _____ I believe that all types of recreational needs and interests should be met through recreation education. The individual should have an opportunity to choose from among social, aesthetic and creative, communicative, "learning," and physical recreational activities within the offerings of what might be called a "community school" in the broadest sense of the word. It is absolutely imperative, of course, that these choices be made according with the student's desire to relate to people. All students are striving for self-realization, and the recreation education program can promise opportunities for both individual expression, as well as for group recreational undertakings. Play seems necessary for people of all ages, and it can assume many different forms. We should not forget that one of its functions is simply personal liberation and release.

C. ____ I believe it is difficult to separate the objectives of recreation education from physical education when physical activities are being considered. Within the schools I recommend a unified approach for health, physical education, recreation education, and dance. In this discussion I am only including those recreational activities that are "physical" in nature. All these leisure activities should be available to all students on a year-round basis. I see recreation education as a legitimate phase of the core curriculum, but later in the day I would include additional recreational opportunities as well as opportunity for relaxation. In a core curriculum so-called extracurricular activities are quite as integral as "spoke and hub" activities. In fact, the word "extra" has now become most misleading.

D. ____ I am inclined to adopt the adoption of the name recreation education for the field. I see advantages in a unified approach whereby the four specialized areas of health, physical education, recreation, and dance (in schools) would provide a variety of experiences that would enable the young person to live a richer, fuller life through superior adjustment to the environment. I believe that education for the worthy use of leisure is basic to the curriculum of the school, a curriculum in which pupil growth, as defined broadly, is all-important. Secondly, play should be conducted in such a way that desirable moral growth will be fostered. Thirdly, over-organized sport competition is not true recreation, since the welfare of the individual is often submerged to the extreme emphasis that is so frequently placed on winning. I believe it is a mistake to confuse the psychological distinction between work and play with the traditional economic distinction generally recognized. All citizens should have ample opportunity to use their free time in a creative and fruitful manner. I do not condemn a person who watches others perform with a high level of skill in any of our cultural recreational activities, including sport, so long as the individual keeps such viewing in a balanced role in personal living.

E. ____ I believe that the role of play and recreation in the development of personality and the "perfectly integrated" individual is looming larger with each passing year, and that such a role has not been fully understood or appreciated in the past. For this reason it seems quite logical to me that education should re-assess the contributions that recreation and play do make in the overall education of the student. That there is a need for further educational research along these lines is self-evident to me. I believe further that we should examine very closely any theories of play and recreation that grant educational possibilities to these activities of people. The self-expression theory of play, for example, suggests that the human's chief need in life is to achieve the satisfaction and accomplishment of self-expression of one's own personality. Here is an explanation that considers quite fully the conception of the human as an organic unity, a total organism. I believe that a person is a purposive being who is striving to achieve those values that are embedded in reality itself. To the extent that we can realize the eternal values through the choice of the right kinds of play and recreation without flouting the moral order in the world, we should be "progressive" enough to disregard a dualistic theory of work and play. Another difficulty that confronts us is differentiating between physical education and recreation. Recreation in its totality has developed to the point where it is now clearly one of our major social institutions. I believe that recreation can make a contribution to the development of an "integrated individual in an integrated society growing in the image of the integrated universe." Humankind today, as I see it, is faced with a "recreational imperative."

F. _____ I believe that there is a radical, logically fundamental difference between statements of what is the case and statements of what ought to be the case. When people express their beliefs about recreation education, their disagreements can be resolved in principle. However, it is logical also that there can be sharing of beliefs (facts, knowledge) with radical disagreement in attitudes. In a democracy, for example, we can conceivably agree on the fact that people of all ages should be involved in wholesome recreational activities of all types, but we can't force people to get actively involved or even to hold a favorable attitude toward such activity. We can demonstrate tenable theory about such recreational involvement, but we cannot prove that a certain attitude toward such activity is the correct one. Thus I can accept evidence that specific types of recreational activity may bring about certain effects or changes in the individual, but my own attitude toward subsequent regular involvement—the values in it for me—is the result of a commitment rather than a prediction.

Category VI

VALUES IN PHYSICAL EDUCATION & EDUCATIONAL SPORT

A. _____ I believe in the concept of total fitness which implies an educational design directed toward the individual's self-realization as a social being. In education, for example, there should be an opportunity for selection of a wide variety of useful human motor performance activities relating to sport, exercise, dance, and play is necessary to provide a sufficient amount of "physical" fitness activity. The introduction of dance, music, and art into physical education can contribute to the person's creative expression. Intramural sports and voluntary physical recreational activities should be stressed. This applies especially to team competitions with particular stress on cooperation and the promotion of friendly competition. Extramural sport competition should be introduced when there is a need. Striving for excellence is important, but it is vital that materialistic influences should be kept out of the educational program. In today's increasingly stressful environment, relaxation techniques should have a place too, as should the concept of education for leisure.

B. _____ I believe that the field of physical education & educational sport should strive to fulfill a role in the general education pattern of the arts and sciences. The goal is total fitness, not only physical fitness, with a balance between activities emphasizing competition and cooperation. The concepts of universal man and universal woman are paramount, but we must allow the individual to choose his or her sport, exercise, and dance activities for himself or herself based on knowledge of self and what knowledge and/or skills he or she would like to possess. We should help the child who is "authentically eccentric" feel at home in the physical education program. It is also important that we find ways for youth to commit themselves to values and people. A person should be able, and be permitted, to select developmental physical activity according to the values he or she wishes to derive from it. This is often difficult in our society today because of the extreme overemphasis placed on winning—being Number 1! Finally, creative movement activities such as modern dance should be stressed, also.

C._____ I believe that education "of the physical" should have primary emphasis in the field of physical education. I am concerned with the development of physical vigor, and such development should have priority over the recreational aspects of sport and physical education. Many people who hold the same educational philosophy as I do recommend that all students in public schools should have a daily period designed to strengthen their muscles and develop their bodily coordination and circulo-respiratory endurance. Sport and physical education must, of course, yield precedence to intellectual education. I give qualified approval to interscholastic, intercollegiate, and interuniversity athletics, since they help with the learning of sportsmanship and desirable social conduct if properly carried out. However, all these objectives, with the possible exception of physical training, are definitely extracurricular and are not part of what we call the regular educational curriculum.

D. _____ I am much more interested in promoting the concept of total fitness rather than physical fitness alone. I believe that sport and physical education should be considered an integral subject in the curriculum. Students should have the opportunity to select a wide variety of useful activities, many of which should help to develop "social intelligence." The activities offered should bring what are considered natural impulses into play. To me, developmental physical activity classes and intramural-recreational sports are much more important to the large majority of students than highly competitive athletics offered at considerable expense for the few. Thus physical education and sport for the "normal" or "special" young man or woman deserves priority if conflicts arise over budgetary allotment, staff availability, and facility use. However, I can still give full support to "educational" competitive sport, because such individual, dual, and/or team activities can provide vital educational experiences for young people if properly conducted.

E. _____ I believe that there is a radical, logically fundamental difference between statements of what is the case and statements of what ought to be the case. When people express their beliefs about physical education and (educational) sport, their disagreements can be resolved in principle. However, it is logical also that there can be sharing of beliefs (facts, knowledge) with radical disagreement in attitudes. In a democracy, for example, we can conceivably agree on the fact that jogging (or bicycling, swimming, walking, etc.) brings about certain circulo-respiratory changes, but we can't force people to get actively involved or even to hold a favorable attitude toward such activity. We can demonstrate tenable theory about the benefit of such physical involvement, therefore, but we cannot prove that a certain attitude toward such activity is the correct one. Thus I may accept evidence that vigorous sport, dance, exercise, and play can bring about certain effects or changes in the organism, but my own attitude toward subsequent regular involvement—the values in it for me—are the result of a commitment rather than a prediction.

F. _____ I am extremely interested in individual personality development. I believe in education "of the physical," and yet I believe in education "through the (medium of the) physical" as well. Accordingly, I see physical education & sport as important, but also occupying a lower rung on the educational ladder. I believe that desirable objectives for physical education and sport would include the development of responsible citizenship and group participation. In competitive sport, I believe that the transfer of training theory is in operation in connection with the development of desirable personality traits (or undesirable traits if the leadership is poor). Participation in highly competitive sport should always serve as a means to a desirable end (often a dubious premise in today's verly emphasized competition).

Note: *Appreciation should be expressed at this point to the following people from whose work phrases and very short quotations were taken for inclusion in the checklist. Inclusion of their names at those particular points in the text did not seem advisable, inasmuch as the particular position or stance may have been instantly recognized: John S. Brubacher, Abraham Kaplan, Morton White, William Barrett, E.A. Burtt, Van Cleve Morris, Ralph Harper, Herbert Spencer, J. Donald Butler, George R. Geiger, Theodore Brameld, John Wild, Harry S. Broudy, James Feibleman, Roy W. Sellars, Isaac L. Kandel, Alfred N. Whitehead, Mortimer J. Adler, Wm. McGucken, Pope Pius XII, Herman H. Horne, Theodore M. Greene, Wm. E. Hocking, and Paul Weiss.*

Answers: *Read only after the question under each six category have been completed. Record your answer to each part of the checklist on the summarizing tally form below.*

I. The Nature of Reality (Metaphysics)

a. Somewhat Progressive (Reconstructionism, Brameld)

b. Analytic (a philosophic method, not a stance))

    c. Existentialistic (atheistic, agnostic, or theistic)

    d. Progressive (Pragmatic Naturalism; EthicalNaturalism)

    e. Traditional (Philosophic Realism, with elements of Naturalistic Realism, Rational Humanism, and positions within Catholic educational philosophy)—Type "B"

    f. Traditional (Philosophic Idealism)—Type "A"

II. Ethics (Axiology)

    a. Traditional / Type "B"

    b. Progressive

    c. Analytic

    d. Existentialistic

    e. Traditional / Type "A"

    f. Somewhat Progressive

III. Educational Aims and Objectives

    a. Existentialistic

    b. Somewhat Progressive

    c. Analytic

    d. Progressive

    e. Traditional / Type "B"

    f. Traditional / Type "A"

IV. The Educative Process (Epistemology)

    a. Traditional / Type "A"

    b. Existentialistic

    c. Progressive

    d. Analytic

    e. Somewhat Progressive

    f. Traditional / Type "B"

V. Recreation

    a. Traditional / Type "B"

    b. Existentialism

    c. Somewhat Progressive

d. Progressive

e. Traditional / Type "A"

f. Analytic

VI. Physical Education & Educational Sport

a. Somewhat Progressive

b. Existentialistic

c. Traditional / Type "B"

d. Progressive

e. Analytic

f. Traditional / Type "A"

Table 1

Summarizing Tally for Self-Evaluation

Note: *For explanation of symbols, please see key below.*

	Prg.	Prg-S.	Exist.	Trd.	Trd-S.	Anal.	
Category I	_____	_____	_____	_____	_____	_____	Metaphysics
Category II	_____	_____	_____	_____	_____	_____	Ethics & Morality
Category III	_____	_____	_____	_____	_____	_____	Educational Objectives
Category IV	_____	_____	_____	_____	_____	_____	Epistemology
Category V	_____	_____	_____	_____	_____	_____	Recreation
Category VI	_____	_____	_____	_____	_____	_____	Phys. Educ. & Educ.Sport
Totals	_____	_____	_____	_____	_____	_____	

KEY: Prg. = *progressive;* **Prg.-S.** = *somewhat progressive;* **Exist.**=*existentialistic;*
  Trd. = *traditional;* **Trd-S** = *strongly traditional;* **Anal.** = *analytic*

Further Instructions:

It should now be possible—keeping in mind the subjectivity of an instrument such as this—to determine your position approximately based on the answers that you have given and tallied on the form immediately above.

At the very least you should be able to tell if you are progressive, traditional, existentialistic, or analytic in your philosophic approach (or stance).

If you discover considerable eclecticism in your overall position or stance—that is, checks that place you on opposite sides of the freedom-constraint spectrum, or some vacillation with checks in the existentialistic or analytic categories—you may wish to analyze your positions or stances more closely to see if your overall position is philosophically defensible.

Keep in mind that your choices under Category I (Metaphysics or Nature of Reality) and Category II (Axiology/Values) are basic and—in all probability—have a strong influence on your subsequent selections.

Now please examine the freedom-constraint spectrum below. Keep in mind that "Existentialistic" is not considered a position or stance as the others are (e.g., Traditional or Philosophic Idealism). Also, if you tend to be "Analytic," this means that your preoccupation is with analysis as opposed to any philosophic/theologic system-building.

Finally, then, after tallying the answers (your "score" above), and keeping in mind that the goal is not to pigeonhole you forever, did this self-evaluation checklist show you to be:

( )   Strongly Progressive—FIVE or SIX checks left of center on the spectrum?

( )   Progressive—FOUR or FIVE checks left of center?

( )   Somewhat Progressive—FOUR checks left of center?

( )   Eclectic—Checks in two or three (?) positions on both the right and left of the spectrum's center?

( )   Somewhat Traditional—FOUR checks right of center?

( )   Traditional—FOUR or FIVE checks right of center?

( ) Strongly Traditional—FIVE or SIX checks right of center?

( ) Existentialistic—FOUR or FIVE checks (including Category
     I) relating to this stance?

( ) Analytic—FOUR or FIVE checks (including Category
     I) relating to this approach to doing philosophy?

Figure 3

The Freedom-Constraint Spectrum

Eclectic*

Existentialistic**   Traditional
(atheistic, agnostic, or theistic)   (Idealism)

Somewhat Progressive   Traditional
(Reconstructionism; Brameld)   (Naturalistc Realism and Communism)

Progressive   Traditional
(Pragmatic Naturalism)   (Rational Humanism)

Strongly Progressive   Strongly Traditional
(Naive Naturalism)   (Scholastic Realism)

ANARCHY   DICTATORSHIP
"the left"   "the right"

Analytic Orientation—a philosophic outlook, actually with ancient origins (as opposed to metaphysical or normative philosophizing), that moved ahead strongly in the twentieth century. The assumption has been that our ordinary language has many defects that need correction. There is concern also with conceptual analysis. Another objective is "the rational reconstruction of the language of science" (Abraham Kaplan). The basic preoccupation is with analysis as opposed to philosophical system-building based on metaphysical and/or normative methodology.

* So-called **eclecticism** is placed in the center because it assumes that the person evaluating himself or herself has selected several positions or stances on opposite sides of the spectrum. Most would argue that eclecticism is philosophically indefensible, while some believe that "patterned eclecticism" (or "reasoned incoherence" as a few have called this position) represents a stance that many of us hold.

** **Existentialistic-Phenomenological Orientation**—a permeating influence rather than a full-blown philosophical position; there are those with either an atheistic, agnostic, or theistic orientation. This position is shown slightly to the left of center because within this "tendency" there is a strong emphasis on individual freedom of choice

ISBN 155395047-X